KNITTED ANIMAL FRIENDS

LOUISE CROWTHER

sewandso

www.sewandso.co.uk

CONTENTS

INTRODUCTION

Welcome to my collection of animal friends, all knitted with one thing in mind: to make them irresistible. We all have a special person in our lives who would love one of these little characters, even if it's ourselves! If you can't choose between a smart fox, or a cheeky raccoon, you could always make them all...

In this book I have gathered all the information you will need from yarn choice to finishing techniques, and kept the patterns concise and clear to make the creation of each animal as enjoyable to knit as the finished toy is to give.

Don't feel that you have to stick to the outfits I have made for each creature. As the animals are all the same size, you can mix and match as much as you like. I have carefully designed each item of clothing so it will fit any of the animals, with little buttoned openings to accommodate all the different sized tails. Why not create Charlotte's coat in a shade of blue for Amelia? Or make your hedgehog a boy with shorts and a striped jumper? You could even make a whole interchangeable wardrobe for one lucky animal.

The patterns in this book are designed for you and your friends and family to enjoy and are for private use only. I can't wait to see photos of your knitted animal friends! Share them using the hashtag #knittedanimalfriends, so that I can enjoy looking at your creations and you can take a look at everyone else's too.

Whatever you choose to knit, I hope that you enjoy the process and cherish your finished animal friend as much as I have loved designing and creating them.

TOOLS AND MATERIALS

YARN

Cotton yarn has always been my favourite yarn for toys. I love the look and feel of cotton, it is non-allergic for most people, incredibly robust and stands up well to being played with.

The animals in this book have all been made using Scheepjes Stonewashed yarn which is a sport weight 78% cotton/22% acrylic mix yarn. Sport weight is slightly thicker than 4-ply but thinner than DK, also sometimes referred to as 5-ply yarn.

All the animals' outfits in this book have been made using Scheepjes Catona and Scheepjes Catona Denim yarns, both these are a 4-ply (fingering) weight 100% cotton yarn.

Although I recommend using the above yarns to achieve the same look and feel as my animals, the patterns will work just as well with other sport weight yarns for the animals and other 4-ply yarns for the outfits. When substituting yarns you need to look for ones with a similar tension/gauge on the ball band as the ones recommended (see below for ball band information).

BALL BAND INFORMATION:

SCHEEPJES STONEWASHED

Available in balls of 50g (1¾oz) = 130m (142yd)

Tension: 24 stitches and 32 rows for a 10 x 10cm (4 x 4in) tension square using 3–3.5mm (US 2½–US 4) needles.

SCHEEPJES CATONA

Available in balls of 50g (1¾oz) = 125m (137yd), 25g (1oz) = 62 (68yd), or 10g (¼oz) = 25m (27yd)

Tension: 26 stitches and 36 rows for a 10 x 10cm (4 x 4in) tension square using 2.75-3.5mm (US 2-US 4) needles.

SCHEEPJES CATONA DENIM

Available in balls of 50g (1¾oz) = 125m (137yd)

Tension: 26 stitches and 36 rows for a 10 x 10cm (4 x 4in) tension square using 3mm (US 2½) needles.

NEEDLES

The animals are all made flat on a pair of straight needles; I like the structure this gives the animals and find working Intarsia and stuffing the toys much easier this way.

You will need a pair of 2.75mm (US 2) straight needles to knit the animals and a selection of 3mm (US 2½) and 3.5mm (US 4) needles to knit their outfits (see patterns), but you may find you need to adjust your needle sizes to achieve the correct tension/gauge.

The outfits are mostly knitted in the round: I prefer to use the 23cm (9in) circular sock needles for these little garments with a set of four double-pointed needles for the sleeves and a pair of straight needles for any back and forth knitting, but you can use whichever method of knitting in the round you are most comfortable with (magic loop, two circular needles, dpns).

BUTTONS

For the animals' eyes I have used 10mm (½in) diameter buttons. For the outfits you can use any buttons with a diameter of about 6–9mm (¼–⅜in). The small buttons I used on the outfits are 6mm (¼in) and the slightly larger wooden buttons are about 9mm (⅜in).

Please bear in mind that if using buttons with a diameter of 6mm (¼in) you may want to make slightly tighter buttonholes (see Essential Notes).

Safety note - *Don't use safety eyes, buttons, beads or glass eyes on toys for children under three years old as they are a potential choking hazard.*

STUFFING

I recommend a synthetic high-loft polyester toy filling for stuffing these animals. It is lovely and soft, holds its shape well and is hand or machine washable on a cool delicates cycle. When stuffing your animal use small pieces, roll and manipulate the body parts in your hands to spread the stuffing evenly and ensure a smooth shape. Tease out any lumps using a blunt tapestry needle carefully inserted through the knitting in the gap between stitches.

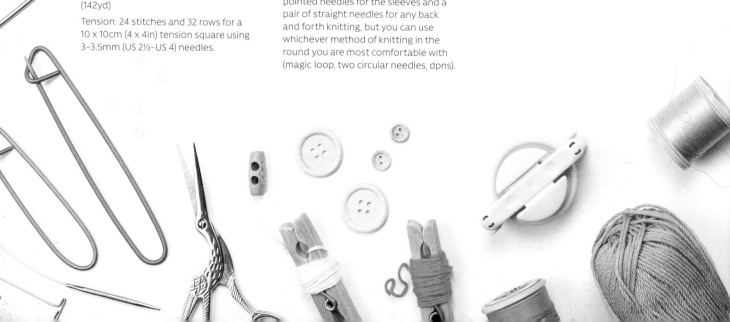

BASIC KIT

In addition to the things on the 'You Will Need' lists in the patterns, these are the other items you need to complete the animals and their outfits. The following is a basic guide:

· Cable needle
· Tapestry needle
· Stitch holders
· Stitch markers
· Removable stitch markers
· Waste yarn
· Sewing needle and thread
· Long sewing needle
· Scissors
· Toy stuffing
· Blocking pins

WASHING

If made using the recommended yarn and stuffed with synthetic toy filling, these animals can either be washed by hand or on a gentle cool cycle in your washing machine. I would recommend reshaping the animals and their clothing whilst still damp.

TIP

The needles listed in the You Will Need lists in each project are the ones that I used for the animals and their outfits, but as a bare minimum you could just use a pair of 2.75mm (US 2), 3mm (US 2½) and 3.5mm (US 4) straight needles, and a set of four 3mm (US 2½) and four 3.5mm (US 4) double-pointed needles.

ABBREVIATIONS

C3B	Slip 2 stitches onto cable needle and hold at back of work, K1, K2 stitches from cable needle
C3F	Slip 1 stitch onto cable needle and hold at front of work, K2, K1 stitch from cable needle
C4B	Slip 2 stitches onto cable needle and hold at back of work, K2, K2 stitches from cable needle
C4F	Slip 2 stitches onto cable needle and hold at front of work, K2, K2 stitches from cable needle
CDD	Central double decrease: slip 2 stitches together knitwise, K1, pass the 2 slipped stitches over
CN	Cable needle
dpn(s)	Double-pointed needle(s)
K	Knit
K2tog	Knit 2 stitches together
K3tog	Knit 3 stitches together
Kfb	Knit 1 stitch through front loop, then knit through back loop
kw	Knitwise
LH	Left-hand
M1	Make 1 stitch: from the front, lift loop between stitches with left needle, knit into back of loop
m1a	Make one away: create a loop by placing right thumb over working yarn, rolling it behind, under, then back up in front of yarn. Place loop onto RH needle
m1l	Make 1 left: from the front, lift loop between stitches with left needle, knit into back of loop
m1pl	Make one purlwise left: from the front, lift loop between stitches with left needle, purl into back loop
m1pr	Make one purlwise right: from the back, lift loop between stitches with left needle, purl into front loop
m1r	Make 1 right: from the back, lift loop between stitches with left needle, knit into front of loop
P	Purl

P2tog	Purl 2 stitches together
P3tog	Purl 3 stitches together
PCDD	Purl central double decrease: slip 1 knitwise, slip 1 knitwise, pass both slipped stitches back onto LH needle, slip 2 stitches together through the back loops and pass them back onto LH needle once again. Purl 3 stitches together
Pfb	Purl 1 stitch through front loop, then purl through back loop
pm	Place marker
PSSO	Pass slipped stitch(es) over
pw	Purlwise
RH	Right-hand
Rnd(s)	Round(s)
rpt	Repeat
rs	Right side
sl1	Slip 1 stitch purlwise
sm	Slip marker
SSK	Slip 2 stitches knitwise one at a time, knit together through back loops
SSP	Slip 2 stitches knitwise one at a time, purl together through back loops
SSSK	Slip 3 stitches knitwise one at a time, knit together through back loops
SSSP	Slip 3 stitches knitwise one at a time, purl together through back loops
St(s)	Stitch(es)
Stocking stitch	Knit all stitches on right side rows, purl all stitches on wrong side rows
ws	Wrong side
wyib	With yarn in back
wyif	With yarn in front
YO	Yarn over

ESSENTIAL NOTES

The best way to avoid potential muddles is to start off correctly, and to be armed with advance knowledge of any particular techniques a knitting pattern might ask for. Please do read the following notes before you begin – they apply to all the patterns and they're not called essential for nothing!

FINISHED SIZE

All of the animals are approximately 40cm (16in) tall (excluding ears).

TENSION

Animal patterns = 29 sts and 47 rows to 10 x 10cm (4 x 4in) over stocking stitch using 2.75mm (US 2) needles.

Outfit patterns = 26 sts and 36 rows to 10 x1 0cm (4 x 4in) over stocking stitch using 3.5mm (US 4) needles.

FOR ALL PATTERNS...

• Cast on using the Long tail cast-on (double cast-on) method (see Techniques: Casting On and Stitches). Leave long tails when you cast on and cast off to sew the parts together, this will make your life easier when sewing up the animals and their outfits.

• Use Mattress stitch (see Techniques: Casting On and Stitches) for sewing up seams (unless stated otherwise) and weave in ends as you go.

• Use the Intarsia technique (see Techniques: Colourwork) for changing yarn across a row; the different yarn colours within a row are indicated in brackets: (A) = use Yarn A, (B) = use Yarn B.

• If you find the central increase stitches on the animal's head too tight to manage, wrap the yarn twice around the needle when knitting or purling the centre stitch on the row below, dropping this extra wrap before making the first central increase on the next row.

• Please bear in mind that if using buttons with a diameter of 6mm (¼in) on the animals' outfits you may want to make slightly tighter buttonholes. To do this, do not work the YO for the buttonhole; instead, on the next row, when you reach where the YO should have been, pick up the loop between the stitches (from front to back) and knit through the front loop. Mark where the YO should be with a stitch marker so you don't forget to pick up the loop on the next row.

STANDARD BODY PARTS

All of the animals are a standard size and shape, and most feature the same basic bodies, arms and legs. The standard patterns for these body parts are given here and referenced throughout the book. Yarn details and any alterations to the patterns are provided with the instructions for each animal, but please feel free to mix and match the different body part styles and vary the colours to create your own unique animals too!

Before you start, please read the Essential Notes at the beginning of this book.

BODY

PLAIN (PHOTO 1)

Using Yarn A and 2.75mm straight needles, cast on 8 sts.

Starting at base:

Row 1 (ws): Purl.

Row 2: [K1, M1] to last st, K1. (15 sts)

Row 3: Purl.

Row 4: [K2, M1] to last st, K1. (22 sts)

Row 5: Purl.

Row 6: [K3, M1] to last st, K1. (29 sts)

Row 7: Purl.

Row 8: [K4, M1] to last st, K1. (36 sts)

Row 9: Purl.

Row 10: [K5, M1] to last st, K1. (43 sts)

Row 11: Purl.

Row 12: [K6, M1] to last st, K1. (50 sts)

Row 13: Purl.

Row 14: [K7, M1] to last st, K1. (57 sts)

Row 15: Purl.

Row 16: [K8, M1] to last st, K1. (64 sts)

Row 17: P20, K10, P4, K10, P20. (The knit stitches on this row mark the leg positions.)

Rows 18-37: Stocking stitch 20 rows.

Row 38: K1, K2tog, K17, CDD, K18, CDD, K17, SSK, K1. (58 sts)

Rows 39-47: Stocking stitch 9 rows.

Row 48: K1, K2tog, K15, CDD, K16, CDD, K15, SSK, K1. (52 sts)

Rows 49-55: Stocking stitch 7 rows.

Row 56: K1, K2tog, K13, CDD, K14, CDD, K13, SSK, K1. (46 sts)

Rows 57-61: Stocking stitch 5 rows.

Row 62: K1, K2tog, K11, CDD, K12, CDD, K11, SSK, K1. (40 sts)

Rows 63-67: Stocking stitch 5 rows.

Row 68: K1, K2tog, K9, CDD, K10, CDD, K9, SSK, K1. (34 sts)

Rows 69-71: Stocking stitch 3 rows.

Row 72: K1, K2tog, K7, CDD, K8, CDD, K7, SSK, K1. (28 sts)

Rows 73-75: Stocking stitch 3 rows.

Row 76: [K1, K2tog] to last st, K1. (19 sts)

Row 77: Purl.

Row 78: K2tog to last st, K1. (10 sts)

Row 79: Purl.

Cut yarn leaving a long tail. Using a tapestry needle, thread tail through the stitches left on needle and pull up tight to gather stitches.

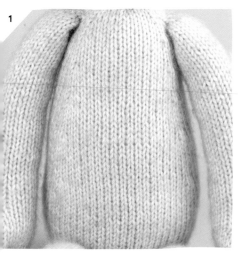

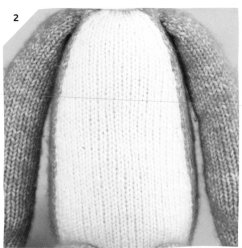

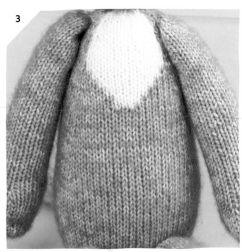

CONTRAST FRONT (PHOTO 2)

Using Yarn A and 2.75mm straight needles, cast on 8 sts.

Rows 1-17: As Rows 1-17 of Standard Body – Plain.

Use the Intarsia technique (see Techniques: Colourwork) for changing yarn across the rows that follow. The different yarn colours in a row are indicated in brackets. (A) = Yarn A. (B) = Yarn B.

Row 18: (A) K21, (B) K22, (A) K21.

Row 19: (A) P21, (B) P22, (A) P21.

Rows 20-37: Rpt last 2 rows 9 more times.

Row 38: (A) K1, K2tog, K16, K2tog, (B) SSK, K18, K2tog, (A) SSK, K16, SSK, K1. (58 sts)

Row 39: (A) P19, (B) P20, (A) P19.

Row 40: (A) K19, (B) K20, (A) K19.

Rows 41-47: Rpt last 2 rows 3 more times, then rpt Row 39 again.

Row 48: (A) K1, K2tog, K14, K2tog, (B) SSK, K16, K2tog, (A) SSK, K14, SSK, K1. (52 sts)

Row 49: (A) P17, (B) P18, (A) P17.

Row 50: (A) K17, (B) K18, (A) K17.

Rows 51-55: Rpt last 2 rows twice more, then rpt Row 49 again.

Row 56: (A) K1, K2tog, K12, K2tog, (B) SSK, K14, K2tog, (A) SSK, K12, SSK, K1. (46 sts)

Row 57: (A) P15, (B) P16, (A) P15.

Row 58: (A) K15, (B) K16, (A) K15.

Rows 59-61: Rpt last 2 rows once more, then rpt Row 57 again.

Row 62: (A) K1, K2tog, K10, K2tog, (B) SSK, K12, K2tog, (A) SSK, K10, SSK, K1. (40 sts)

Row 63: (A) P13, (B) P14, (A) P13.

Row 64: (A) K13, (B) K14, (A) K13.

Rows 65-67: Rpt last 2 rows once more, then rpt Row 63 again.

Row 68: (A) K1, K2tog, K8, K2tog, (B) SSK, K10, K2tog, (A) SSK, K8, SSK, K1. (34 sts)

Row 69: (A) P11, (B) P12, (A) P11.

Row 70: (A) K11, (B) K12, (A) K11.

Row 71: (A) P11, (B) P12, (A) P11.

Row 72: (A) K1, K2tog, K6, K2tog, (B) SSK, K8, K2tog, (A) SSK, K6, SSK, K1. (28 sts)

Row 73: (A) P9, (B) P10, (A) P9.

Row 74: (A) K9, (B) K10, (A) K9.

Row 75: (A) P9, (B) P10, (A) P9.

Row 76: (A) [K1, K2tog] 3 times, (B) [K1, K2tog] 3 times, K1, (A) [K2tog, K1] 3 times. (19 sts)

Row 77: (A) P6, (B) P7, (A) P6.

Continue in Yarn A only.

Row 78: K2tog to last st, K1. (10 sts)

Row 79: Purl.

Cut yarn leaving a long tail. Using a tapestry needle, thread tail through the stitches left on needle and pull up tight to gather stitches.

CHEST BLAZE (PHOTO 3)

Using Yarn A and 2.75mm straight needles, cast on 8 sts.

Rows 1-48: As Rows 1-48 of Standard Body – Plain.

Rows 49-51: Stocking stitch 3 rows.

Use the Intarsia technique (see Techniques: Colourwork) for changing yarn across the rows that follow. The different yarn colours in a row are indicated in brackets. (A) = Yarn A. (B) = Yarn B.

Row 52: (A) K25, (B) K2, (A) K25.

Row 53: (A) P24, (B) P4, (A) P24.

Row 54: (A) K24, (B) K4, (A) K24.

Row 55: (A) P23, (B) P6, (A) P23.

Row 56: (A) K1, K2tog, K13, CDD, K4, (B) K6, (A) K4, CDD, K13, SSK, K1. (46 sts)

Row 57: (A) P19, (B) P8, (A) P19.

Row 58: (A) K19, (B) K8, (A) K19.

Row 59: (A) P18, (B) P10, (A) P18.

Row 60: (A) K18, (B) K10, (A) K18.

Row 61: (A) P17, (B) P12, (A) P17.

Row 62: (A) K1, K2tog, K11, CDD, (B) K12, (A) CDD, K11, SSK, K1. (40 sts)

Row 63: (A) P14, (B) P12, (A) P14.

Row 64: (A) K14, (B) K12, (A) K14.

Rows 65-67: Rpt last 2 rows once more, then rpt Row 63 again.

Row 68: (A) K1, K2tog, K9, K2tog, (B) SSK, K8, K2tog, (A) SSK, K9, SSK, K1. (34 sts)

Row 69: (A) P12, (B) P10, (A) P12.

Row 70: (A) K12, (B) K10, (A) K12.

Row 71: (A) P12, (B) P10, (A) P12.

Row 72: (A) K1, K2tog, K7, K2tog, (B) SSK, K6, K2tog, (A) SSK, K7, SSK, K1. (28 sts)

Row 73: (A) P10, (B) P8, (A) P10.

Row 74: (A) K10, (B) K8, (A) K10.

Row 75: (A) P10, (B) P8, (A) P10.

Row 76: (A) [K1, K2tog] 3 times, K1, (B) [K2tog, K1] twice, K2tog, (A) [K1, K2tog] 3 times, K1. (19 sts)

Row 77: (A) P7, (B) P5, (A) P7.

Continue in Yarn A only.

Row 78: K2tog to last st, K1. (10 sts)

Row 79: Purl.

Cut yarn leaving a long tail. Using a tapestry needle, thread tail through the stitches left on needle and pull up tight to gather stitches.

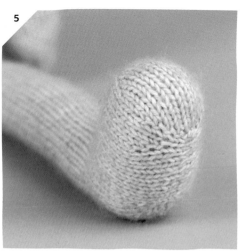

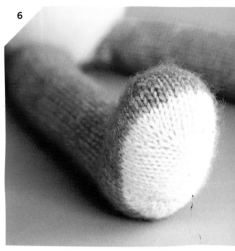

PATCH (PHOTO 4)

Using Yarn A and 2.75mm straight needles, cast on 8 sts.

Rows 1-29: As Rows 1-29 of Standard Body – Plain.

Use the Intarsia technique (see Techniques: Colourwork) for changing yarn across the rows that follow. The different yarn colours in a row are indicated in brackets. (A) = Yarn A. (B) = Yarn B.

Row 30: (A) K7, (B) K7, (A) K50.

Row 31: (A) P48, (B) P10, (A) P6.

Row 32: (A) K5, (B) K12, (A) K47.

Row 33: (A) P46, (B) P13, (A) P5.

Row 34: (A) K5, (B) K13, (A) K46.

Row 35: (A) P45, (B) P15, (A) P4.

Row 36: (A) K4, (B) K15, (A) K45.

Row 37: (A) P45, (B) P15, (A) P4.

Row 38: (A) K1, K2tog, K1, (B) K15, (A) K1, CDD, K18, CDD, K17, SSK, K1. (58 sts)

Row 39: (A) P41, (B) P14, (A) P3.

Row 40: (A) K3, (B) K14, (A) K41.

Row 41: (A) P40, (B) P15, (A) P3.

Row 42: (A) K3, (B) K15, (A) K40.

Row 43: (A) P40, (B) P14, (A) P4.

Row 44: (A) K4, (B) K14, (A) K40.

Row 45: (A) P40, (B) P14, (A) P4.

Row 46: (A) K3, (B) K15, (A) K40.

Row 47: (A) P41, (B) P14, (A) P3.

Row 48: (A) K1, K2tog, (B) K14, (A) K1, CDD, K16, CDD, K15, SSK, K1. (52 sts)

Row 49: (A) P37, (B) P13, (A) P2.

Row 50: (A) K2, (B) K10, (A) K40.

Row 51: (A) P41, (B) P9, (A) P2.

Row 52: (A) K2, (B) K9, (A) K41.

Row 53: (A) P41, (B) P9, (A) P2.

Row 54: (A) K3, (B) K7, (A) K42.

Rows 55-79: As Rows 55-79 of Standard Body – Plain.

Cut yarn leaving a long tail. Using a tapestry needle, thread tail through the stitches left on needle and pull up tight to gather stitches.

ARMS (MAKE 2)

Using Yarn A and 2.75mm straight needles, cast on 14 sts.

Row 1 (ws): Purl.

Row 2: K1, [M1, K2] 6 times, M1, K1. (21 sts)

Rows 3-47: Stocking stitch 45 rows.

Row 48: K10, m1r, K1, m1l, K10. (23 sts)

Row 49: Purl.

Row 50: K11, m1r, K1, m1l, K11. (25 sts)

Rows 51-55: Stocking stitch 5 rows.

Row 56: K7, K2tog twice, CDD, SSK twice, K7. (19 sts)

Rows 57-61: Stocking stitch 5 rows.

Row 62: K1, K2tog 4 times, K1, SSK 4 times, K1. (11 sts)

Row 63: Purl.

Cut yarn leaving a long tail. Using a tapestry needle, thread tail through the stitches left on needle and pull up tight to gather stitches.

LEGS (MAKE 2)

PLAIN (PHOTO 5)

Using Yarn A and 2.75mm straight needles, cast on 20 sts.

Row 1 (ws): Purl.

Row 2: K1, M1, K6, [K2, M1] twice, K8, M1, K1. (24 sts)

Row 3: Purl.

Row 4: [K1, M1] twice, K6, [K1, M1] twice, K3, [K1, M1] twice, K6, [K1, M1] twice, K1. (32 sts)

Row 5: Purl.

Row 6: [K2, M1] twice, K5, [K2, M1] twice, K4, [K2, M1] twice, K5, [K2, M1] twice, K2. (40 sts)

Row 7: Purl.

Row 8: [K3, M1] twice, K4, [K3, M1] twice, K5, [K3, M1] twice, K4, [K3, M1] twice, K3. (48 sts)

Rows 9-13: Stocking stitch 5 rows.

Row 14: K19, SSK, K6, K2tog, K19. (46 sts)

Row 15: Purl.

Row 16: K19, SSK, K4, K2tog, K19. (44 sts)

Row 17: Purl.

Row 18: K19, SSK, K2, K2tog, K19. (42 sts)

Row 19: Purl.

Row 20: K11, [K8, SSK, K2tog, K8] and cast off these 18 sts as you work them, K to end. (22 sts)

Row 21: P10, P2tog, P10. (21 sts)

Rows 22-89: Stocking stitch 68 rows.

Cast off.

CONTRAST FOOT PAD (PHOTO 6)

As Standard Legs – Plain, but cast on and work Rows 1-8 using Yarn B, then work remainder using Yarn A.

THE ANIMALS

GEORGE
THE DOG

Dressed for adventure, George has his pockets full
of dog biscuits and a neck scarf to catch any drool
if he gets too excited. He's wearing his best jeans
and striped sweater, and he's ready for anything!

YOU WILL NEED

FOR GEORGE'S BODY

• Scheepjes Stonewashed
(50g/130m; 78% cotton/22%
acrylic) yarn in the
following shades:

 - *Yarn A Cream (Moonstone
 801), 2 balls*

 - *Yarn B Black (Black Onyx 803),
 1 ball*

• 2.75mm (US 2) straight needles

• Toy stuffing

• 2 x 10mm (½in) buttons

• Scrap piece of 4-ply yarn
for embroidering nose

FOR GEORGE'S OUTFIT

• Scheepjes Catona (10g/25m,
25g/62m or 50g/125m;
100% cotton) yarn in the
following shades:

 - *Yarn A Pale Grey (Light Silver
 172), 1 x 25g ball*

 - *Yarn B Cream (Old Lace 130),
 1 x 25g ball*

 - *Yarn C Deep Red (Rosewood
 258), 1 x 10g ball*

• Scheepjes Catona Denim
(50g/125m; 100% cotton)
yarn in the following shade:

 - *Yarn D Denim Blue (Dark Blue
 Mix 150), 1 x 50g ball*

• 3mm (US 2½) straight needles

• 3mm (US 2½) circular
needle (23cm/9in length)

• Set of four 3mm (US 2½)
double-pointed needles

• 3.5mm (US 4) straight needles

• 3.5mm (US 4) circular
needle (23cm/9in length)

• Set of four 3.5mm (US 4)
double-pointed needles

• Cable needle

• Waste yarn

• 7 small buttons

Before you start, please read the Essential Notes at the beginning of this book.

DOG PATTERN

HEAD

Starting at neck:

Using Yarn A and 2.75mm straight needles, cast on 11 sts.

Row 1 (ws): Purl.

Row 2: [K1, M1] to last st, K1. (21 sts)

Row 3: Purl.

Row 4: [K2, M1] to last st, K1. (31 sts)

Row 5: Purl.

Row 6: [K1, m1l, K14, m1r] twice, K1. (35 sts)

Row 7: Purl.

Row 8: [K1, m1l, K16, m1r] twice, K1. (39 sts)

Row 9: P19, m1pl, P1, m1pr, P19. (41 sts)

Row 10: [K1, m1l, K19, m1r] twice, K1. (45 sts)

Row 11: P22, m1pl, P1, m1pr, P22. (47 sts)

Row 12: [K1, m1l, K22, m1r] twice, K1. (51 sts)

Row 13: P25, m1pl, P1, m1pr, P25. (53 sts)

Row 14: K26, m1r, K1, m1l, K26. (55 sts)

Row 15: Purl.

Row 16: [K1, m1l, K26, m1r] twice, K1. (59 sts)

Row 17: Purl.

Row 18: (A) K29, sl1, K12, (B) K6, (A) K11.

Row 19: (A) P10, (B) P9, (A) P40.

Row 20: (A) K29, sl1, K9, (B) K11, (A) K9.

Row 21: (A) P9, (B) P11, (A) P39.

Row 22: (A) K29, sl1, K8, (B) K13, (A) K8.

Row 23: (A) P8, (B) P13, (A) P7, PCDD, P28. (57 sts)

Row 24: (A) K27, CDD, K6, (B) K14, (A) K7. (55 sts)

Row 25: (A) P7, (B) P14, (A) P5, PCDD, P26. (53 sts)

Row 26: (A) K25, CDD, K4, (B) K14, (A) K7. (51 sts)

Row 27: (A) P7, (B) P14, (A) P3, PCDD, P24. (49 sts)

Row 28: (A) K1, K2tog, K20, CDD, K3, (B) K13, (A) K4, SSK, K1. (45 sts)

Row 29: (A) P6, (B) P13, (A) P2, PCDD, P21. (43 sts)

Row 30: (A) K20, CDD, K1, (B) K13, (A) K6. (41 sts)

Row 31: (A) P6, (B) P12, (A) P23.

Row 32: (A) K1, K2tog, K17, sl1, K2, (B) K12, (A) K3, SSK, K1. (39 sts)

Row 33: (A) P5, (B) P12, (A) P22.

Row 34: (A) K19, sl1, K3, (B) K11, (A) K5.

Row 35: (A) P5, (B) P11, (A) P23.

Row 36: (A) K1, K2tog, K16, sl1, K3, (B) K11, (A) K2, SSK, K1. (37 sts)

Row 37: (A) P4, (B) P10, (A) P23.

Row 38: (A) K18, sl1, K5, (B) K8, (A) K5.

Continue in Yarn A only.

Row 39: Purl.

Row 40: K1, K2tog, K3, K2tog 4 times, K3, CDD, K3, SSK 4 times, K3, SSK, K1. (25 sts)

Row 41: Purl.

Row 42: K1, K2tog 5 times, CDD, SSK 5 times, K1. (13 sts)

Row 43: Purl.

Cast off.

EARS (MAKE 2)

Using Yarn B and 2.75mm straight needles, cast on 31 sts.

Row 1 (ws): Purl.

Rows 2-7: Stocking stitch 6 rows.

Row 8: [K6, K2tog, SSK, K5] twice, K1. (27 sts)

Rows 9-11: Stocking stitch 3 rows.

Row 12: [K5, K2tog, SSK, K4] twice, K1. (23 sts)

Rows 13-15: Stocking stitch 3 rows.

Row 16: [K4, K2tog, SSK, K3] twice, K1. (19 sts)

Rows 17-19: Stocking stitch 3 rows.

Row 20: [K3, K2tog, SSK, K2] twice, K1. (15 sts)

Rows 21-23: Stocking stitch 3 rows.

Row 24: [K2, K2tog, SSK, K1] twice, K1. (11 sts)

Row 25: Purl.

Row 26: [K1, K2tog, SSK] twice, K1. (7 sts)

Cut yarn leaving a long tail. Using a tapestry needle, thread tail through the stitches left on needle and pull up tight to gather stitches.

TAIL

Using Yarn A and 2.75mm straight needles, cast on 18 sts.

Row 1 (ws): Purl.

Rows 2-7: Stocking stitch 6 rows.

Row 8: K1, K2tog, K12, SSK, K1. (16 sts)

Rows 9-15: Stocking stitch 7 rows.

Row 16: K1, K2tog, K10, SSK, K1. (14 sts)

Rows 17-31: Stocking stitch 15 rows.

Row 32: K1, K2tog, K8, SSK, K1. (12 sts)

Rows 33-37: Stocking stitch 5 rows.

Row 38: K1, K2tog, K6, SSK, K1. (10 sts)

Rows 39-41: Stocking stitch 3 rows.

Row 42: K1, K2tog, K4, SSK, K1. (8 sts)

Row 43: Purl.

Row 44: K1, K2tog twice, SSK, K1. (5 sts)

Row 45: Purl.

Cut yarn leaving a long tail. Using a tapestry needle, thread tail through the stitches left on needle and pull up tight to gather stitches.

BODY

Work as Standard Body – Patch (see Standard Body Parts).

ARMS (MAKE 2)

Work as Standard Arms (see Standard Body Parts).

LEGS (MAKE 2)

Work as Standard Legs – Contrast Foot Pad (see Standard Body Parts).

MAKING UP

Follow the instructions in the techniques section (see Techniques: Making Up Your Animal).

OUTFIT PATTERNS

STRIPY SWEATER

The sweater is worked top down, with raglan sleeves and no seams. The top half is worked back and forth in rows, and the body and sleeves are worked in the round.

Using Yarn A and 3.5mm straight needles, cast on 36 sts.

Row 1 (ws): Purl.

Rows 2-4: Stocking stitch 3 rows.

Row 5: Cast on 3 sts using Purl cast-on method (see Techniques: Casting On and Stitches), P9, pm, P12, pm, P6, pm, purl to end. (39 sts)

Row 6: P3, K1, m1l, [knit to marker, m1r, sm, K1, m1l] 3 times, knit to last 4 sts, m1r, K1, P3. (47 sts)

From this point work in a stripe rpt of 2 rows Yarn B and 2 rows Yarn A, starting with Yarn B.

Row 7 (buttonhole row): Purl to last 2 sts, YO, P2tog.

Row 8: P3, K1, m1l, [knit to marker, m1r, sm, K1, m1l] 3 times, knit to last 4 sts, m1r, K1, P3. (55 sts)

Row 9: Purl.

Rows 10-12: Rpt last 2 rows once more, then rpt Row 8 again. (71 sts)

Row 13 (buttonhole row): As Row 7.

Rows 14-18: Rpt Rows 8-12. (95 sts)

Row 19 (buttonhole row): As Row 7.

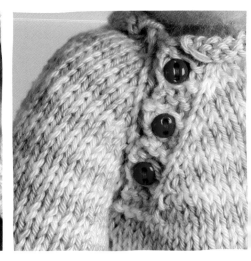

Rows 20-23: Rpt Rows 8-9 twice. (111 sts)

Row 24: Transfer sts to a 3.5mm circular needle, P3, K1, m1l, [knit to marker, m1r, sm, K1, m1l] 3 times, knit to last 4 sts, m1r, K1, slip the last 3 sts (without working them) onto a cable needle. (119 sts)

Join to work in the round:

Rnd 25: Position cable needle behind first 3 sts on left-hand needle, place marker for beginning of round, knit first st on left-hand needle together with first st on cable needle, rpt for next 2 sts, K29, sm, K1 (front), place next 25 sts (without working them) onto waste yarn (sleeve), remove marker, K32, remove marker, K1 (back), place next 25 sts (without working them) onto waste yarn (sleeve). (66 sts)

Rnd 26: K1, m1l, knit to marker, m1r, sm, K2, m1l, knit to last st, m1r, K1. (70 sts)

Rnds 27-29: Knit 3 rnds.

Rnds 30-41: Rpt Rnds 26-29 3 more times. (82 sts)

Rnds 42-44: Knit 3 rnds.

Change to a 3mm circular needle and Yarn A.

Rnd 45: Knit.

Rnd 46: Purl.

Rnds 47-48: Rpt last 2 rnds once more.

Cast off.

SLEEVES

Starting at under arm, slip the 25 sts held on waste yarn for 1 sleeve evenly onto three 3.5mm dpns and rejoin yarn.

The sleeves are worked in a stripe rpt of 2 rows Yarn A and 2 rows Yarn B, starting with Yarn A.

Using fourth dpn, start knitting in the round.

Rnds 1-3: Knit 3 rnds.

Rnd 4: K1, m1l, knit to last st, m1r, K1. (27 sts)

Rnds 5-11: Knit 7 rnds.

Rnd 12: K1, m1l, knit to last st, m1r, K1. (29 sts)

Rnds 13-20: Knit 8 rnds.

Change to a set of 3mm dpns and Yarn A.

Rnd 21: Knit.

Rnd 22: Purl.

Rnds 23-24: Rpt last 2 rnds once more.

Cast off.

Rpt for second sleeve.

MAKING UP

1. If necessary, close hole under arm with a couple of stitches.

2. Block sweater.

3. Sew buttons in place on right-hand button band, matching them up with the buttonholes.

DENIM JEANS

The jeans are worked top down with no seams except for the pockets, which are made separately and sewn on afterwards. The top part is worked back and forth with a button band down the back and some short row shaping for the bottom. The lower half and legs are worked in the round.

Using Yarn D and 3mm straight needles, cast on 52 sts.

Row 1 (ws): Knit.

Row 2: Knit.

Row 3 (buttonhole row): Knit to last 3 sts, K2tog, YO, K1.

Rows 4-5: Knit 2 rows.

Change to 3.5mm straight needles.

Row 6: [K1, K1fb] 11 times, K1fb 3 times, K1, K1fb 4 times, [K1, K1fb] 10 times, K2. (80 sts)

Row 7: K2, P8, turn.

Row 8: YO, knit to end.

Row 9: K2, P8, SSP, P2, turn.

Row 10: YO, knit to end.

Row 11: K2, P11, SSP, P2, turn.

Row 12: YO, knit to end.

Row 13: K2, P14, SSP, P2, turn.

Row 14: YO, knit to end.

Row 15: K2, P17, SSP, purl to last 2 sts, K2.

Row 16: K10, turn.

Row 17: YO, purl to last 2 sts, K2.

Row 18: K10, K2tog, K2, turn.

Row 19 (buttonhole row): YO, purl to last 3 sts, P2tog, YO, K1.

Row 20: K13, K2tog, K2, turn.

Row 21: YO, purl to last 2 sts, K2.

Row 22: K16, K2tog, K2, turn.

Row 23: YO, purl to last 2 sts, K2.

Row 24: K19, K2tog, knit to end.

Row 25: K2, purl to last 2 sts, K2.

Row 26: Knit.

Row 27 (buttonhole row): K2, purl to last 3 sts, P2tog, YO, K1.

Row 28: Knit.

Row 29: K2, purl to last 2 sts, K2.

Rows 30-31: Rpt last 2 rows once more.

Row 32: Transfer sts to a 3.5mm circular needle and knit to last 2 sts, slip the last 2 sts (without working them) onto a cable needle.

Join to work in the round:

Rnd 33: Position the cable needle behind the first 2 sts on the left-hand needle, knit first st on left-hand needle together with first st on cable needle, place marker for beginning of round, knit next st on left-hand needle together with remaining st on cable needle, knit to end. (78 sts)

Rnds 34-37: Knit 4 rnds.

Rnd 38: K1, m1l, knit to last st, m1r, K1. (80 sts)

Rnds 39-40: Knit 2 rnds.

Rnd 41: K1, m1l, knit to last st, m1r, K1. (82 sts)

Rnd 42: K40, m1r, K2, m1l, knit to end. (84 sts)

Rnd 43: K1, m1l, knit to last st, m1r, K1. (86 sts)

Rnd 44: Knit.

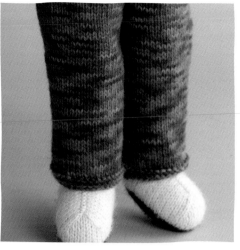

Rnd 45: K1, m1l, K41, m1r, K2, m1l, K41, m1r, K1. (90 sts)

Rnd 46: Knit.

Rnd 47: K1, m1l, K43, m1r, K2, m1l, K43, m1r, K1. (94 sts)

Rnd 48: Knit.

Divide for legs:

Rnd 49: K47 (right leg), place next 47 sts (without working them) onto waste yarn (left leg).

RIGHT LEG

Rnds 50-53: Knit 4 rnds.

Rnd 54: SSK, K22, K2tog, knit to end. (45 sts)

Rnds 55-63: Knit 9 rnds.

Rnd 64: SSK, K20, K2tog, knit to end. (43 sts)

Rnds 65-73: Knit 9 rnds.

Rnd 74: SSK, K18, K2tog, knit to end. (41 sts)

Rnds 75-83: Knit 9 rnds.

Rnd 84: SSK, K16, K2tog, knit to end. (39 sts)

Rnds 85-97: Knit 13 rnds.

Change to 3mm circular needle.

Rnd 98: Knit.

Rnd 99: Purl.

Rnds 100-103: Rpt last 2 rnds twice more.

Cast off.

LEFT LEG

Rnd 49: Transfer sts from waste yarn onto 3.5mm circular needle, rejoin yarn and knit 1 rnd, placing marker for beginning of rnd.

Rnds 50-53: Knit 4 rnds.

Rnd 54: K21, SSK, K22, K2tog. (45 sts)

Rnds 55-63: Knit 9 rnds.

Rnd 64: K21, SSK, K20, K2tog. (43 sts)

Rnds 65-73: Knit 9 rnds.

Rnd 74: K21, SSK, K18, K2tog. (41 sts)

Rnds 75-83: Knit 9 rnds.

Rnd 84: K21, SSK, K16, K2tog. (39 sts)

Rnds 85-97: Knit 13 rnds.

Change to 3mm circular needle.

Rnd 98: Knit.

Rnd 99: Purl.

Rnds 100-103: Rpt last 2 rows twice more.

Cast off.

POCKET (MAKE 2)

Using Yarn D and 3mm straight needles, cast on 11 sts.

Row 1 (ws): Knit.

Change to 3.5mm straight needles.

Rows 2-10: Stocking stitch 9 rows.

Row 11: Purl to last st, sl1.

Row 12: Wyib slip 2 sts, pass the first slipped stitch over the second, cast off 1 st, knit to last st, sl1. (9 sts)

Row 13: Wyif slip 2 sts, pass the first slipped stitch over the second, cast off 1 st pw, purl to last st, sl1. (7 sts)

Rows 14-15: Rpt last 2 rows once more. (3 sts)

Row 16: Wyib slip 2 sts, pass the first slipped stitch over the second, sl1. (2 sts)

Row 17: Wyif slip 2 sts, pass the first slipped stitch over the second. (1 st)

Cut yarn leaving a long tail. Using a tapestry needle, thread tail through the stitch left on needle and pull up tight to secure.

MAKING UP

1. If necessary, close hole with a couple of stitches where the 2 legs join.

2. Block jeans and pockets.

3. Position pockets on back of jeans, with each innermost top corner of the pocket approximately 3cm (1¼in) in from edge of back opening and 4cm (1½in) down from top of waist. Pin in place. Sew around 3 sides leaving top of pocket open.

4. Sew buttons in place on left-hand button band down back of jeans, matching them up with the buttonholes.

BANDANA

Using Yarn C and 3.5mm straight needles, cast on 36 sts.

Row 1 (ws): Knit.

Row 2: Knit.

Row 3 (buttonhole row): K7, YO, K2tog, knit to end.

Row 4: Knit.

Row 5: Cast off 19 sts, knit to end. (17 sts)

Row 6: Knit to last 2 sts, K2tog. (16 sts)

Row 7: Knit.

Rows 8-31: Rpt last 2 rows 12 more times. (4 sts)

Rows 32-59: Knit 28 rows.

Cast off.

MAKING UP

1. Block bandana.

2. Sew a button on the opposite tab to buttonhole, on the right side of work and about 2.5cm (1in) from cast-off end.

BELLA
THE CAT

Because she sometimes feels the cold, Bella likes
to dress warmly in her favourite sweater and skirt.
If she finds herself at a loose end, she entertains
herself by chasing the pompoms on her scarf.

YOU WILL NEED

FOR BELLA'S BODY

- Scheepjes Stonewashed (50g/130m; 78% cotton/22% acrylic) yarn in the following shades:

  - *Yarn A Mustard (Yellow Jasper 809), 2 balls*

  - *Yarn B Cream (Moonstone 801), 1 ball*

- 2.75mm (US 2) straight needles

- Toy stuffing

- 2 x 10mm (½in) buttons

- Scrap piece of 4-ply yarn for embroidering nose

FOR BELLA'S OUTFIT

- Scheepjes Catona (10g/25m, 25g/62m or 50g/125m; 100% cotton) yarn in the following shades:

  - *Yarn A Pale Pink (Powder Pink 238), 1 x 50g ball*

  - *Yarn B Purple (Amethyst 240), 1 x 50g ball*

  - *Yarn C Dark Pink (Coral Rose 398), 1 x 10g ball*

  - *Yarn D Cream (Old Lace 130), 1 x 25g ball*

- 3mm (US 2½) straight needles

- 3mm (US 2½) circular needle (23cm/9in length)

- Set of four 3mm (US 2½) double-pointed needles

- 3.5mm (US 4) straight needles

- 3.5mm (US 4) circular needle (23cm/9in length)

- Set of four 3.5mm (US 4) double-pointed needles

- Cable needle

- Waste yarn

- 9 small buttons

- 35mm (1⅜in) pompom maker

Before you start, please read the Essential Notes at the beginning of this book.

CAT PATTERN

HEAD

Starting at neck:

Using 2.75mm straight needles and Yarn A, cast on 11 sts.

Row 1 (ws): Purl.

Row 2: [K1, M1] to last st, K1. (21 sts)

Row 3: Purl.

Row 4: [K2, M1] to last st, K1. (31 sts)

Row 5: Purl.

Row 6: K1, m1l, knit to last st, m1r, K1. (33 sts)

Row 7: Purl.

Row 8: [K1, m1l, K15, m1r] twice, K1. (37 sts)

Row 9: P18, m1pl, P1, m1pr, P18. (39 sts)

Row 10: (A) K1, m1l, K16, (B) [m1l, K1] twice, m1l, (A) K1, (B) [m1r, K1] twice, m1r, (A) K16, m1r, K1. (47 sts)

Row 11: (A) P18, (B) P1, m1pr, P4, (A) K1, (B) P4, m1pl, P1, (A) P18. (49 sts)

Row 12: (A) K1, m1l, K17, (B) K1, m1l, K11, m1r, K1, (A) K17, m1r, K1. (53 sts)

Row 13: (A) P19, (B) P1, m1pr, P13, m1pl, P1, (A) P19. (55 sts)

Row 14: (A) K19, (B) K1, m1l, K15, m1r, K1, (A) K19. (57 sts)

Row 15: (A) P19, (B) P19, (A) P19.

Row 16: (A) K1, m1l, K18, (B) K19, (A) K18, m1r, K1. (59 sts)

Row 17: (A) P20, (B) P19, (A) P20.

Row 18: (A) K20, (B) K19, (A) K20.

Row 19: (A) P20, (B) P3tog, P13, SSSP, (A) P20. (55 sts)

Row 20: (A) K20, (B) SSSK, K9, K3tog, (A) K20. (51 sts)

Row 21: (A) P20, (B) P3tog, P5, SSSP, (A) P20. (47 sts)

Row 22: (A) K20, (B) SSSK, K1, K3tog, (A) K20. (43 sts)

Row 23: (A) P20, (B) P3, (A) P20.

Row 24: (A) K20, (B) K3, (A) K20.

Row 25: (A) P20, (B) P3, (A) P20.

Continue in Yarn A only.

Row 26: K21, sl1, K21.

Row 27: Purl.

Row 28: K1, K2tog, K18, sl1, K18, SSK, K1. (41 sts)

Row 29: Purl.

Row 30: K20, sl1, K20.

Row 31: Purl.

Row 32: K1, K2tog, K17, sl1, K17, SSK, K1. (39 sts)

Row 33: Purl.

Row 34: K19, sl1, K19.

Row 35: Purl.

Row 36: K1, K2tog, K16, sl1, K16, SSK, K1. (37 sts)

Row 37: Purl.

Row 38: K18, sl1, K18.

Row 39: Purl.

Row 40: K1, K2tog, K3, K2tog 4 times, K3, CDD, K3, SSK 4 times, K3, SSK, K1. (25 sts)

Row 41: Purl.

Row 42: K1, K2tog 5 times, CDD, SSK 5 times, K1. (13 sts)

Row 43: Purl.

Cast off.

EARS (MAKE 2)

Using 2.75mm straight needles and Yarn A, cast on 21 sts.

Row 1 (ws): (A) P8, (B) P5, (A) P8.

Row 2: (A) K8, (B) [K1, M1] 4 times, K1, (A) K8. (25 sts)

Row 3: (A) P8, (B) P9, (A) P8.

Row 4: (A) K5, K2tog, K1, (B) SSK, K5, K2tog, (A) K1, SSK, K5. (21 sts)

Row 5: (A) P7, (B) P7, (A) P7.

Row 6: (A) K4, K2tog, K1, (B) SSK, K3, K2tog, (A) K1, SSK, K4. (17 sts)

Row 7: (A) P6, (B) P5, (A) P6.

Row 8: (A) K3, K2tog, K1, (B) SSK, K1, K2tog, (A) K1, SSK, K3. (13 sts)

Row 9: (A) P5, (B) P3, (A) P5.

Row 10: (A) K2, K2tog, SSK, (B) K1, (A) K2tog, SSK, K2. (9 sts)

Continue in Yarn A only.

Row 11: Purl.

Row 12: K1, K2tog, sl1 kw, K2tog, PSSO, SSK, K1. (5 sts)

Cut yarn leaving a long tail. Using a tapestry needle, thread tail through the stitches left on needle and pull up tight to gather stitches.

TAIL

Using 2.75mm straight needles and Yarn A, cast on 12 sts.

Row 1 (ws): Purl.

Rows 2–79: Stocking stitch 78 rows.

Change to Yarn B.

Rows 80–86: Stocking stitch 7 rows.

Cut yarn leaving a long tail. Using a tapestry needle, thread tail through the stitches left on needle and pull up tight to gather stitches.

BODY

Work as Standard Body – Chest Blaze (see Standard Body Parts).

ARMS (MAKE 2)

Work as Standard Arms (see Standard Body Parts).

LEGS (MAKE 2)

Work as Standard Legs – Contrast Foot Pad (see Standard Body Parts).

MAKING UP

Follow the instructions in the techniques section (see Techniques: Making Up Your Animal).

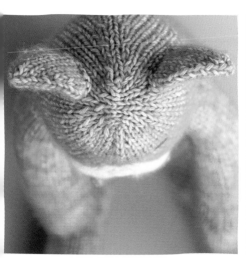

OUTFIT PATTERNS

SWEET SWEATER

The sweater is worked top down, with raglan sleeves and no seams. The top half is worked back and forth in rows, and the body and sleeves are worked in the round.

Using Yarn A and 3.5mm straight needles, cast on 36 sts.

Row 1 (ws): Purl.

Rows 2–4: Stocking stitch 3 rows.

Row 5: Cast on 3 sts using Purl cast-on method (see Techniques: Casting On and Stitches), P9, pm, P12, pm, P6, pm, purl to end. (39 sts)

Row 6: P3, K1, m1l, [knit to marker, m1r, sm, K1, m1l] twice, K2, K2tog, (K1, YO) twice, K1, SSK, K2, m1r, sm, K1, m1l, knit to last 4 sts, m1r, K1, P3. (47 sts)

Row 7 (buttonhole row): Purl to last 2 sts, YO, P2tog.

Row 8: P3, K1, m1l, [knit to marker, m1r, sm, K1, m1l] twice, K2, K2tog, K1, YO, K3, YO, K1, SSK, K2, m1r, sm, K1, m1l, knit to last 4 sts, m1r, K1, P3. (55 sts)

Row 9: Purl.

Row 10: P3, K1, m1l, [knit to marker, m1r, sm, K1, m1l] twice, K2, K2tog, K1, YO, K5, YO, K1, SSK, K2, m1r, sm, K1, m1l, knit to last 4 sts, m1r, K1, P3. (63 sts)

Row 11: Purl.

Row 12: P3, K1, m1l, [knit to marker, m1r, sm, K1, m1l] twice, K2, K2tog, K1, YO, K7, YO, K1, SSK, K2, m1r, sm, K1, m1l, knit to last 4 sts, m1r, K1, P3. (71 sts)

Row 13 (buttonhole row): P35, place marker (pattern marker), purl to last 2 sts, YO, P2tog.

Row 14: P3, K1, m1l, [knit to marker, m1r, sm, K1, m1l] twice, knit to pattern marker, (K1, K2tog, K1, YO) 2 times, (K1, YO, K1, SSK) twice, K1, knit to marker, m1r, sm, K1, m1l, knit to last 4 sts, m1r, K1, P3. (79 sts)

Row 15: Purl.

Row 16: P3, K1, m1l, [knit to marker, m1r, sm, K1, m1l] twice, knit to pattern marker, K4, K2tog, K1, YO, K3, YO, K1, SSK, K4, knit to marker, m1r, sm, K1, m1l, knit to last 4 sts, m1r, K1, P3. (87 sts)

Row 17: Purl.

Row 18: P3, K1, m1l, [knit to marker, m1r, sm, K1, m1l] twice, knit to pattern marker, K3, K2tog, K1, YO, K5, YO, K1, SSK, K3, knit to marker, m1r, sm, K1, m1l, knit to last 4 sts, m1r, K1, P3. (95 sts)

Row 19 (buttonhole row): Purl to last 2 sts, YO, P2tog.

Row 20: P3, K1, m1l, [knit to marker, m1r, sm, K1, m1l] twice, knit to pattern marker, K2, K2tog, K1, YO, K7, YO, K1, SSK, K2, knit to marker, m1r, sm, K1, m1l, knit to last 4 sts, m1r, K1, P3. (103 sts)

Row 21: Purl.

Rows 22–23: Rpt Rows 14–15 once more. (111 sts)

Row 24: Transfer sts to a 3.5mm circular needle, P3, K1, m1l, [knit to marker, m1r, sm, K1, m1l] twice, knit to pattern marker, K4, K2tog, K1, YO, K3, YO, K1, SSK, K4, knit to marker, m1r, sm, K1, m1l, knit to last 4 sts, m1r, K1, slip the last 3 sts (without working them) onto a cable needle. (119 sts)

Join to work in the round:

Rnd 25: Position the cable needle behind the first 3 sts on the LH needle and knit them together: insert the RH needle in the first stitch on the LH needle, then in the first stitch on the cable needle, knit both stitches together; rpt for the next 2 sts, K29, sm, K1 (back), without working them place next 25 sts onto waste yarn (sleeve), remove marker, K32, remove marker, K1 (front), without working them place next 25 sts onto waste yarn (sleeve). (66 sts)

Rnd 26: K1, m1l, knit to marker, m1r, sm, K2, m1l, knit to pattern marker, K3, K2tog, K1, YO, K5, YO, K1, SSK, K3, knit to last st, m1r, K1. (70 sts)

Rnd 27: Knit.

Rnd 28: Knit to pattern marker, K2, K2tog, K1, YO, K7, YO, K1, SSK, K2, knit to end.

Rnd 29: Knit.

Rnd 30: K1, m1l, knit to marker, m1r, sm, K2, m1l, knit to pattern marker, (K1, K2tog, K1, YO) twice, (K1, YO, K1, SSK) twice, K1, knit to last st, m1r, K1. (74 sts)

Rnd 31: Knit.

Rnd 32: Knit to pattern marker, K4, K2tog, K1, YO, K3, YO, K1, SSK, K4, knit to end.

Rnd 33: Knit.

Rnds 34–41: Rpt Rnds 26-33 once more. (82 sts)

Rnd 42: Knit to pattern marker, K3, K2tog, K1, YO, K5, YO, K1, SSK, K3, knit to end.

Rnds 43–44: Rpt Rnds 27-28 once more.

Change to 3mm circular needle.

Rnd 45: Knit.

Rnd 46: Purl.

Rnds 47–48: Rpt last 2 rnds once more.

Cast off.

SLEEVES

Starting at under arm, slip the 25 sts held on waste yarn for one sleeve onto three 3.5mm dpns and rejoin yarn.

Using fourth dpn, start knitting in the round.

Rnds 1-3: Knit 3 rnds.

Rnd 4: K1, m1l, knit to last st, m1r, K1. (27 sts)

Rnds 5-11: Knit 7 rnds.

Rnd 12: As Rnd 4. (29 sts)

Rnd 13: Knit.

Rnd 14: K9, K2, K2tog, (K1, YO) twice, K1, SSK, K2, K9.

Rnd 15: Knit.

Rnd 16: K8, K2, K2tog, K1, YO, K3, YO, K1, SSK, K2, K8.

Rnd 17: Knit.

Rnd 18: K7, K2, K2tog, K1, YO, K5, YO, K1, SSK, K2, K7.

Rnd 19: Knit.

Rnd 20: K6, K2, K2tog, K1, YO, K7, YO, K1, SSK, K2, K6.

Change to a set of 3mm dpns.

Rnd 21: Knit.

Rnd 22: Purl.

Rnds 23-24: Rpt last 2 rnds once more.

Cast off.

Repeat for second sleeve.

MAKING UP

1. If necessary, close hole under arm with a couple of stitches.

2. Block sweater.

3. Sew buttons in place on left-hand button band, matching them up with the buttonholes.

SKIRT

The skirt is worked from the bottom up, back and forth with a small seam and button band down the back.

Using Yarn B and 3mm straight needles, cast on 193 sts.

Row 1 (ws): *K5, turn, K3tog, turn, sl1wyif; rep from * to last 3 sts, K3. (117 sts)

Rows 2-3: Knit 2 rows.

Change to 3.5mm straight needles.

Rows 4-21: Stocking stitch 18 rows.

Row 22: [K1, K2tog] to end. (78 sts)

Row 23-24: Knit 2 rows.

Row 25: Cast on 1 st, K2, purl to last st, K1. (79 sts)

Row 26: Cast on 1 st, knit to end. (80 sts)

Row 27: K2, purl to last 2 sts, K2.

Row 28: Knit.

Rows 29-30: Rpt the last 2 rows once more.

Row 31 (buttonhole row): K1, YO, SSP, purl to last 2 sts, K2.

Row 32: Knit.

Row 33: K2, purl to last 2 sts, K2.

Rows 34-38: Rpt last 2 rows twice more, then rpt Row 24 again.

Row 39 (buttonhole row): K1, YO, SSP, purl to last 2 sts, K2.

Row 40: Knit.

Row 41: K2, purl to last 2 sts, K2.

Row 42: [K1, K2tog] 12 times, K2tog 5 times, [K1, K2tog] 11 times, K1. (52 sts)

Change to 3mm straight needles.

Row 43-46: Knit 4 rows.

Row 47 (buttonhole row): K1, YO, K2tog, knit to end.

Cast off.

MAKING UP

1. Block skirt.

2. Sew centre back edges together, starting at the hem and ending at the bottom of the button band.

3. Sew buttons in place on left-hand button band, matching them up with the buttonholes.

SHOE LACE SCARF

Using 3.5mm dpns and Yarn B, cast on 4 sts.

Make an i-cord (see Techniques: Casting On and Stitches, Making i-cord), 72cm/30in (190 rows) long.

Using Yarn C, make a pompom approximately 35mm (1⅜in) diameter. Repeat to make 2.

MAKING UP

1. Sew a pompom onto each end of i-cord.

2. Wrap the scarf loosely twice around the cat's neck and tie in a bow at the side, leaving pompom ends to dangle at the front.

FRENCH KNICKERS

Using Yarn D, follow the pattern for the French Knickers (see Shoes and Accessories).

NOAH
THE HORSE

Nothing slows Noah down – he's only got one gear and that's gallop! He therefore needs a practical outfit like this T-shirt and dungarees. Perfect for getting into, and out of, scrapes.

YOU WILL NEED

FOR NOAH'S BODY
- Scheepjes Stonewashed (50g/130m; 78% cotton/22% acrylic) yarn in the following shades:

  - *Yarn A* Brown (Boulder Opal 804), 2 balls

  - *Yarn B* Cream (Moonstone 801), 1 ball

- 2.75mm (US 2) straight needles
- Toy stuffing
- 2 x 10mm (½in) buttons
- Scrap piece of 4-ply yarn for embroidering nostrils

FOR NOAH'S OUTFIT
- Scheepjes Catona Denim (50g/125m; 100% cotton) yarn in the following shade:

  - *Yarn A* Denim Blue (Dark Blue Mix 150), 2 x 50g

- Scheepjes Catona (10g/25m, 25g/62m or 50g/125m; 100% cotton) yarn in the following shades:

  - *Yarn B* Light Blue (Baby Blue 509), 1 x 25g ball

  - *Yarn C* Cream (Old Lace 130), 1 x 25g ball

- 3mm (US 2½) straight needles
- 3mm (US 2½) circular needle (23cm/9in length)
- Set of four 3mm (US 2½) double-pointed needles
- 3.5mm (US 4) straight needles
- 3.5mm (US 4) circular needle (23cm/9in length)
- Set of four 3.5mm (US 4) double-pointed needles
- Cable needle
- Waste yarn
- 15 small buttons

Before you start, please read the Essential Notes at the beginning of this book.

HORSE PATTERN

HEAD

Starting at neck:

Using Yarn A and 2.75mm straight needles, cast on 11 sts.

Row 1 (ws): Purl.

Row 2: [K1, M1] to last st, K1. (21 sts)

Row 3: Purl.

Row 4: [K2, M1] to last st, K1. (31 sts)

Row 5: Purl.

Row 6: K1, m1l, K13, m1r, K3, m1l, K13, m1r, K1. (35 sts)

Row 7: Purl.

Row 8: K1, m1l, K15, m1r, K3, m1l, K15, m1r, K1. (39 sts)

Row 9: P18, m1pl, P3, m1pr, P18. (41 sts)

Row 10: K1, m1l, K18, m1r, K3, m1l, K18, m1r, K1. (45 sts)

Row 11: P21, m1pl, P3, m1pr, P21. (47 sts)

Row 12: K1, m1l, K21, m1r, K3, m1l, K21, m1r, K1. (51 sts)

Row 13: P24, m1pl, P3, m1pr, P24. (53 sts)

Row 14: K25, m1r, K3, m1l, K25. (55 sts)

Row 15: (A) P25, (B) [m1pr, P1] 3 times, [m1pl, P1] twice, m1pl, (A) P25. (61 sts)

Row 16: (A) K1, m1l, K24, (B) K1, m1l, K9, m1r, K1, (A) K24, m1r, K1. (65 sts)

Row 17: (A) P26, (B) P1, m1pr, P11, m1pl, P1, (A) P26. (67 sts)

Row 18: (A) K26, (B) K1, m1l, K13, m1r, K1, (A) K26. (69 sts)

Row 19: (A) P26, (B) P1, m1pr, P15, m1pl, P1, (A) P26. (71 sts)

Row 20: (A) K26, (B) K1, m1l, K17, m1r, K1, (A) K26. (73 sts)

Row 21: (A) P26, (B) P21, (A) P26.

Row 22: (A) K26, (B) K21, (A) K26.

Rows 23–25: Rpt last 2 rows once more, then rpt Row 21 again.

Row 26: (A) K26, (B) SSK, K17, K2tog, (A) K26. (71 sts)

Row 27: (A) P26, (B) P3tog, P13, SSSP, (A) P26. (67 sts)

Row 28: (A) K1, K2tog, K23, (B) SSSK, K9, K3tog, (A) K23, SSK, K1. (61 sts)

Row 29: (A) P25, (B) P3tog, P5, SSSP, (A) P25. (57 sts)

Row 30: (A) K25, (B) SSSK, K1, K3tog, (A) K25. (53 sts)

Row 31: (A) P23, SSP, (B) P3, (A) P2tog, P23. (51 sts)

Row 32: (A) K1, K2tog, K19, K2tog, (B) K3, (A) SSK, K19, SSK, K1. (47 sts)

Row 33: (A) P20, SSP, (B) P3, (A) P2tog, P20. (45 sts)

Row 34: (A) K19, K2tog, (B) K3, (A) SSK, K19. (43 sts)

Row 35: (A) P18, SSP, (B) P3, (A) P2tog, P18. (41 sts)

Row 36: (A) K1, K2tog, K14, K2tog, (B) K3, (A) SSK, K14, SSK, K1. (37 sts)

Row 37: (A) P17, (B) P3, (A) P17.

Row 38: (A) K17, (B) K3, (A) K17.

Row 39: (A) P17, (B) P3, (A) P17.

Row 40: (A) K1, K2tog, K3, K2tog 4 times, K3, (B) K3, (A) K3, SSK 4 times, K3, SSK, K1. (27 sts)

Row 41: (A) P12, (B) P3, (A) P12.

Continue in Yarn A only.

Row 42: K1, K2tog 5 times, K1, sl1 kw, K2tog, PSSO, K1, SSK 5 times, K1. (15 sts)

Row 43: Purl.

Cast off.

EARS (MAKE 2)

Using Yarn A and 2.75mm straight needles, cast on 14 sts.

Row 1 (ws): Purl.

Row 2: K5, [K1, M1] 3 times, knit to end. (17 sts)

Rows 3-9: Stocking stitch 7 rows.

Row 10: [K3, K2tog, SSK] twice, K3. (13 sts)

Row 11: Purl.

Row 12: K1, [K1, K2tog, SSK] twice, K2. (9 sts)

Row 13: Purl.

Row 14: K1, K2tog, sl1 kw, K2tog, PSSO, SSK, K1. (5 sts)

Row 15: Purl.

Row 16: Knit.

Cut yarn leaving a long tail. Using a tapestry needle, thread tail through the stitches left on needle and pull up tight to gather stitches.

MANE

Using Yarn B and 2.75mm dpns, cast on 4 sts for each i-cord (see Techniques: Casting On and Stitches, Making i-cord).

Make 14 i-cords, 8 rows long.

TAIL

Using Yarn B and 2.75mm dpns, cast on 4 sts for each i-cord (see Techniques: Casting On and Stitches, Making i-cord).

Make 2 i-cords 45 rows long.

Make 1 i-cord 40 rows long.

Make 1 i-cord 35 rows long

Make 1 i-cord 30 rows long.

BODY

Work as Standard Body – Plain (see Standard Body Parts).

ARMS (MAKE 2)

Work as Standard Arms (see Standard Body Parts).

LEGS (MAKE 2)

Work as Standard Legs – Plain (see Standard Body Parts).

MAKING UP

Follow the instructions in the techniques section (see Techniques: Making Up Your Animal).

OUTFIT PATTERNS

DENIM DUNGAREES

The dungarees are worked from the bottom up with no seams, except for the pocket which is made separately and sewn on afterwards. The legs and bottom part of the body are worked in the round, the top half is worked back and forth with a button band opening at the back and with some short row shaping for the bottom.

LEFT LEG

Using Yarn A and a set of four 3mm dpns, cast on 39 sts.

Divide stitches evenly onto three dpns. Use the fourth dpn to start knitting in the round.

Rnd 1: Purl.

Rnd 2: Knit.

Rnds 3–5: Rpt last 2 rnds once more, then rpt Rnd 1 again.

Change to 3.5mm circular needle, place marker for beginning of rnd.

Rnds 6–18: Knit 13 rnds.

Rnd 19: K1, m1l, K16, m1r, knit to end. (41 sts)

Rnds 20–28: Knit 9 rnds.

Rnd 29: K1, m1l, K18, m1r, knit to end. (43 sts)

Rnds 30–38: Knit 9 rnds.

Rnd 39: K1, m1l, K20, m1r, knit to end. (45 sts)

Rnds 40–48: Knit 9 rnds.

Rnd 49: K1, m1l, K22, m1r, knit to end. (47 sts)

Rnds 50–55: Knit 6 rnds.

Cut yarn leaving a long tail to weave in later and place sts onto waste yarn.

RIGHT LEG

Using Yarn A and a set of four 3mm dpns, cast on 39 sts.

Divide stitches evenly onto three dpns. Use the fourth dpn to start knitting in the round.

Rnd 1: Purl.

Rnd 2: Knit.

Rnds 3–5: Rpt last 2 rnds once more, then rpt Rnd 1 again.

Change to 3.5mm circular needle, place marker for beginning of rnd.

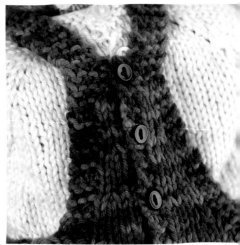

Rnds 6–18: Knit 13 rnds.

Rnd 19: K22, m1l, K16, m1r, K1. (41 sts)

Rnds 20–28: Knit 9 rnds.

Rnd 29: K22, m1l, K18, m1r, K1. (43 sts)

Rnds 30–38: Knit 9 rnds.

Rnd 39: K22, m1l, K20, m1r, K1. (45 sts)

Rnds 40–48: Knit 9 rnds.

Rnd 49: K22, m1l, K22, m1r, K1. (47 sts)

Rnds 50–55: Knit 6 rnds.

Join legs:

Working back from the stitch with the cut tail end, transfer the stitches from the waste yarn onto the LH end of the circular needle (photo 1). (94 sts)

Rnds 56–57: Knit 2 rnds.

Rnd 58: SSK, K43, K2tog, SSK, knit to last 2 sts, K2tog. (90 sts)

Rnd 59: Knit.

Rnd 60: SSK, K41, K2tog, SSK, knit to last 2 sts, K2tog. (86 sts)

Rnd 61: Knit.

Rnd 62: SSK, knit to last 2 sts, K2tog. (84 sts)

Rnd 63: K40, K2tog, SSK, knit to end. (82 sts)

Rnd 64: SSK, knit to last 2 sts, K2tog. (80 sts)

Rnds 65–66: Knit 2 rnds.

Rnd 67: SSK, knit to last 2 sts, K2tog. (78 sts)

Rnds 68–71: Knit 4 rnds.

Rnd 72: Knit to end of rnd, remove marker, K1.

The dungarees are now worked back and forth in rows.

Row 73 (ws): K2, P18, K3, P34, K3, P18, pick up and knit 2 sts from WS of beginning of row as follows: wyib place RH needle up through the purl bump directly below the first stitch on LH needle and knit, dropping the purl loop off the needle. Rpt for second stitch. (80 sts)

Row 74: Knit.

Row 75: K2, P18, K3, P34, K3, P18, K2.

Rows 76–77: Rpt last 2 rows once more.

Row 78 (buttonhole row): Knit to last 3 sts, SSK, YO, K1.

Row 79: As Row 75.

Rows 80–81: Rpt Rows 74-75.

Row 82: K19, turn.

Row 83: YO, P17, K2.

Row 84: K16, turn.

Row 85: YO, P14, K2.

Row 86: K13, turn.

Row 87: YO, P11, K2.

Row 88: K13, [K2tog, K2] 3 times, knit to end.

Row 89: K2, P17, turn.

Row 90: YO, K19.

Row 91 (buttonhole row): K1, YO, SSP, P13, turn.

Row 92: YO, K16.

Row 93: K2, P11, turn.

Row 94: YO, K13.

Row 95: K2, P11, [SSP, P2] twice, SSP, K3, P34, K3, purl to last 2 sts, K2.

Row 96: K6, K2tog, K10, K2tog, K3, SSK, K5, SSK, K16, K2tog, K5, K2tog, K3, SSK, K10, SSK, K6. (72 sts)

Row 97: K2, P5, K20, P18, K20, P5, K2.

Row 98 (buttonhole row): Knit to last 3 sts, SSK, YO, K1.

Row 99: As Row 97.

Row 100: Knit.

Row 101: As Row 97.

Row 102: K5, K2tog, K3, place the 9 sts just worked on hold (left back), cast off 14 sts, K3, SSK, K14, K2tog, K3, place the last 22 sts just worked on hold (front bib), cast off 14 sts, K3, SSK, K5 (right back). (40 sts)

The dungarees are now worked in 3 separate parts.

RIGHT BACK

Row 103: K2, P4, K3.

Row 104: Knit.

Row 105: K2, P4, K3.

Row 106 (buttonhole row): Knit to last 3 sts, SSK, YO, K1.

Row 107: K2, P4, K3.

Row 108: K3, SSK, K4. (8 sts)

Row 109: K2, P3, K3.

Row 110: Knit.

Rows 111–113: Rpt Rows 109–110 once more, then rpt Row 109 again.

Row 114 (buttonhole row): K3, SSK twice, YO, K1. (7 sts)

Row 115: K2, P2, K3.

Row 116: Knit.

Rows 117–119: Rpt Rows 115–116 once more, then rpt Row 115 again.

Row 120: K3, SSK, K2. (6 sts)

Row 121: Knit.

Row 122 (buttonhole row): K3, SSK, YO, K1.

Row 123: Cast off 2 sts, knit to end. (4 sts)

Rows 124–153: Knit 30 rows.

Row 154: K2tog, SSK. (2 sts)

Cut yarn leaving a short tail. Using a tapestry needle, thread tail through the stitches left on needle and draw up. Weave in tail on back of strap.

FRONT BIB

Place the middle 22 sts onto 3.5mm straight needles and rejoin yarn.

Row 103 (ws): K3, purl to last 3 sts, K3.

Row 104: Knit.

Rows 105–107: Rpt Rows 103–104 once more, then rpt Row 103 again.

Row 108: K3, SSK, knit to last 5 sts, K2tog, K3. (20 sts)

Rows 109–120: Rpt Rows 103–108 twice more. (16 sts)

Row 121: Knit.

Row 122 (buttonhole row): K2, YO, K2tog, K8, SSK, YO, K2.

Row 123: Knit.

Cast off.

LEFT BACK

Place the remaining 9 sts onto 3.5mm straight needles and rejoin yarn.

Row 103 (ws): K3, purl to last 2 sts, K2.

Row 104: Knit.

Rows 105–107: Rpt the last 2 rows once more, then rpt Row 103 again.

Row 108: Knit to last 5 sts, K2tog, K3. (8 sts)

Rows 109–120: Rpt Rows 103-108 twice more. (6 sts)

Rows 121–123: Knit 3 rows.

Row 124: Cast off 2 sts, knit to end. (4 sts)

Rows 125–153: Knit 29 rows.

Row 154: K2tog, SSK. (2 sts)

Cut yarn leaving a short tail. Using a tapestry needle, thread tail through the stitches left on needle and draw up. Weave in tail on back of strap.

POCKET

Using Yarn A and 3mm straight needles, cast on 10 sts.

Row 1 (ws): Knit.

Change to 3.5mm straight needles.

Rows 2–11: Stocking stitch 10 rows.

Cast off.

MAKING UP

1. If necessary, close hole where the 2 legs join with a couple of stitches.

2. Block dungarees and pocket.

3. Position pocket in centre of front bib, pin in place. Sew around 3 sides leaving top of pocket open.

4. Sew buttons in place on left-hand button band and at the end of each strap (RS), matching them up with the buttonholes.

5. Sew 2 buttons on the garter strip band on each side of the dungarees (see photo).

T-SHIRT

The T-shirt is worked top down, with raglan short sleeves and no seams. The top half is worked back and forth in rows with a button band opening at the back, and the body and sleeves are worked in the round.

The button band is worked in Yarn B throughout using the Intarsia method (see Techniques: Colourwork).

Using 3mm straight needles and Yarn B, cast on 31 sts.

Row 1 (ws): Knit.

Row 2 (buttonhole row): K1, YO, K2tog, knit to end.

Row 3: Knit.

Row 4: K3, [K1, K1fb, K1] to last 4 sts, K4. (39 sts)

Change to 3.5mm straight needles.

The T-shirt is now worked in a stripe pattern of 2 rows Yarn B and 2 rows Yarn C, starting with Yarn C. The button bands (first and last 3 sts on each row) are worked in Yarn B throughout.

Row 5: (B) K3, (C) P5, pm, P6, pm, P12, pm, P6, pm, P4, (B) K3.

Row 6: (B) K3, (C) [knit to marker, m1r, sm, K1, m1l] 4 times, knit to last 3 sts, (B) K3. (47 sts)

Row 7: K3, purl to last 3 sts, K3.

Row 8: [Knit to marker, m1r, sm, K1, m1l] 4 times, knit to end. (55 sts)

Row 9: (B) K3, (C) purl to last 3 sts, (B) K3.

Row 10 (buttonhole row): (B) K1, YO, K2tog, (C) [knit to marker, m1r, sm, K1, m1l] 4 times, knit to last 3 sts, (B) K3. (63 sts)

Row 11: As Row 7.

Row 12: As Row 8. (71 sts)

Row 13: As Row 9.

Row 14: As Row 6. (79 sts)

Rows 15–20: Rpt Rows 7–10 once more, then rpt Rows 7–8 again. (103 sts)

Row 21: As Row 9.

Row 22: Transfer sts to a 3.5mm circular needle, (B) K3, (C) [knit to marker, m1r, sm, K1, m1l] 4 times, knit to last 3 sts, slip the last 3 sts (without working them) onto a cable needle. (111 sts)

Join to work in the round:

From this point the T-shirt is worked in a stripe pattern of 2 rows Yarn B and 2 rows Yarn C, beginning with Yarn B and without the button band.

Rnd 23: Position cable needle behind first 3 sts on LH needle, place marker for beginning of round, knit first st on LH needle together with first st on cable needle, rpt for next 2 sts, knit to marker, remove marker, K1, m1a (right back), without working them place next 23 sts onto waste yarn (sleeve), remove marker, m1a, knit to marker, remove marker, K1, m1a (front), without working them place next 23 sts onto waste yarn (sleeve), remove marker, m1a, knit to end (left back). (66 sts)

Rnd 24: K17, pm, K33, pm, knit to end.

Rnd 25: [Knit to marker, m1r, sm, K2, m1l] twice, knit to end. (70 sts)

Rnds 26–28: Knit 3 rnds.

Rnds 29–36: Rpt Rnds 25-28 twice more. (78 sts)

Rnd 37–38: Knit 2 rnds.

Change to 3mm circular needle and Yarn B.

Rnd 39: Knit.

Rnd 40: Purl.

Rnds 41–42: Rpt last 2 rnds once more.

Cast off.

SLEEVES

Starting at under arm, slip the 23 sts held on waste yarn for one sleeve evenly onto three 3.5mm dpns and rejoin yarn.

Using the fourth dpn, start knitting in the round.

The sleeves are worked in a stripe rpt of 2 rows Yarn B and 2 rows Yarn C, starting with Yarn B.

Rnd 1: Pick up and knit 1 stitch from under arm, knit to end, pick up and knit 1 stitch from under arm. (25 sts)

Rnds 2–4: Knit 3 rnds.

Change to a set of 3mm dpns and Yarn B.

Rnd 5: Knit.

Rnd 6: Purl.

Rnds 7–8: Rpt last 2 rows once more.

Cast off.

Repeat for second sleeve.

MAKING UP

1. If necessary, close hole under arm with a couple of stitches.

2. Block T-shirt.

3. Sew buttons in place on right-hand button band, matching them up with the buttonholes.

DOROTHY
THE MOUSE

Gentle Dorothy takes great care of her friends when
they visit – almost as much care as she puts into
choosing her co-ordinating shrug and shoes, lovely
ruffle tunic and capri pants with button trim.

YOU WILL NEED

FOR DOROTHY'S BODY
• Scheepjes Stonewashed
(50g/130m; 78% cotton/22%
acrylic) yarn in the
following shade:

- **Yarn A** *Pale Grey (Crystal
Quartz 814), 2 balls*

• 2.75mm (US 2) straight needles

• Toy stuffing

• 2 x 10mm (½in) buttons

• Scrap piece of 4-ply yarn
for embroidering nose

FOR DOROTHY'S OUTFIT
• Scheepjes Catona (10g/25m,
25g/62m or 50g/125m;
100% cotton) yarn in the
following shades:

- **Yarn A** *Cream (Old Lace 130),
1 x 50g ball*

- **Yarn B** *Light Brown (Moon
Rock 254), 1 x 50g ball*

- **Yarn C** *Peach (Sweet
Mandarin 523), 1 x 50g ball*

• 3mm (US 2½) straight needles

• 3mm (US 2½) circular
needle (23cm/9in length)

• Set of four 3mm (US 2½)
double-pointed needles

• 3.5mm (US 4) straight needles

• 3.5mm (US 4) circular
needle (23cm/9in length)

• Set of four 3.5mm (US 4)
double-pointed needles

• Cable needle

• Waste yarn

• 16 small buttons

Before you start, please read the Essential Notes at the beginning of this book.

MOUSE PATTERN

HEAD

Starting at neck:

Using Yarn A and 2.75mm straight needles, cast on 11 sts.

Row 1 (ws): Purl.

Row 2: [K1, M1] to last st, K1. (21 sts)

Row 3: Purl.

Row 4: [K2, M1] to last st, K1. (31 sts)

Row 5: Purl.

Row 6: [K1, m1l, K14, m1r] twice, K1. (35 sts)

Row 7: Purl.

Row 8: [K1, m1l, K16, m1r] twice, K1. (39 sts)

Row 9: P19, m1pl, P1, m1pr, P19. (41 sts)

Row 10: [K1, m1l, K19, m1r] twice, K1. (45 sts)

Row 11: P22, m1pl, P1, m1pr, P22. (47 sts)

Row 12: [K1, m1l, K22, m1r] twice, K1. (51 sts)

Row 13: P25, m1pl, P1, m1pr, P25. (53 sts)

Row 14: K26, m1r, K1, m1l, K26. (55 sts)

Row 15: Purl.

Row 16: [K1, m1l, K26, m1r] twice, K1. (59 sts)

Row 17: Purl.

Row 18: K29, sl1, K29.

Row 19: Purl.

Row 20: K28, CDD, K28. (57 sts)

Row 21: Purl.

Row 22: K27, CDD, K27. (55 sts)

Row 23: Purl.

Row 24: K26, CDD, K26. (53 sts)

Row 25: Purl.

Row 26: K25, CDD, K25. (51 sts)

Row 27: Purl.

Row 28: K1, K2tog, K21, CDD, K21, SSK, K1. (47 sts)

Row 29: Purl.

Row 30: K22, CDD, K22. (45 sts)

Row 31: Purl.

Row 32: K1, K2tog, K18, CDD, K18, SSK, K1. (41 sts)

Row 33: Purl.

Row 34: K19, CDD, K19. (39 sts)

Row 35: Purl.

Row 36: K1, K2tog, K16, sl1, K16, SSK, K1. (37 sts)

Row 37: Purl.

Row 38: K18, sl1, K18.

Row 39: Purl.

Row 40: K1, K2tog, K3, K2tog 4 times, K3, CDD, K3, SSK 4 times, K3, SSK, K1. (25 sts)

Row 41: Purl.

Row 42: K1, K2tog 5 times, CDD, SSK 5 times, K1. (13 sts)

Row 43: Purl.

Cast off.

EARS (MAKE 2)

Using Yarn A and 2.75mm straight needles, cast on 25 sts.

Row 1 (ws): Purl.

Row 2: K7, M1, K2, [M1, K1] 8 times, K1, M1, K7. (35 sts)

Rows 3-7: Stocking stitch 5 rows.

Row 8: [K7, K2tog, SSK, K6] twice, K1. (31 sts)

Rows 9-11: Stocking stitch 3 rows.

Row 12: [K6, K2tog, SSK, K5] twice, K1. (27 sts)

Row 13: Purl.

Row 14: [K5, K2tog, SSK, K4] twice, K1. (23 sts)

Row 15: Purl.

Row 16: [K4, K2tog, SSK, K3] twice, K1. (19 sts)

Row 17: [P3, SSP, P2tog, P2] twice, P1. (15 sts)

Cut yarn leaving a long tail. Using a tapestry needle, thread tail through the stitches left on needle and pull up tight to gather stitches.

TAIL

Using Yarn A and 2.75mm straight needles, cast on 16 sts.

Row 1 (ws): Purl.

Rows 2-7: Stocking stitch 6 rows.

Row 8: [K1, K2tog, K2, SSK, K1] twice. (12 sts)

Rows 9-15: Stocking stitch 7 rows.

Row 16: [K1, K2tog, K1, SSK] twice. (8 sts)

Rows 17-77: Stocking stitch 61 rows.

Row 78: K1, K2tog 3 times, K1. (5 sts)

Row 79: Purl.

Cut yarn leaving a long tail. Using a tapestry needle, thread tail through the stitches left on needle and pull up tight to gather stitches.

BODY

Work as Standard Body - Plain (see Standard Body Parts).

ARMS (MAKE 2)

Work as Standard Arms (see Standard Body Parts).

LEGS (MAKE 2)

Work as Standard Legs – Plain (see Standard Body Parts).

MAKING UP

Follow the instructions in the techniques section (see Techniques: Making Up Your Animal).

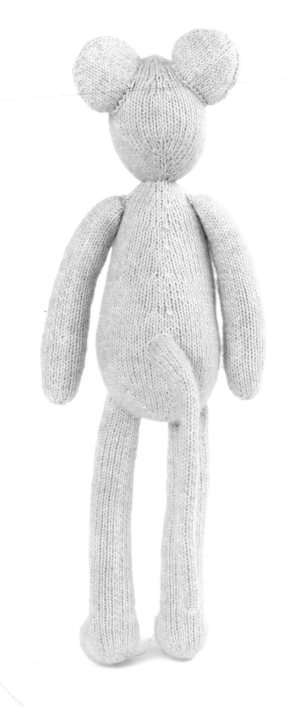

OUTFIT PATTERNS

RUFFLE TUNIC

The tunic is worked top down, seamlessly and back and forth, with raglan sleeves and a button band down the back.

Using Yarn A and 3mm straight needles, cast on 31 sts.

Row 1 (ws): Knit.

Row 2 (buttonhole row): K1, YO, K2tog, knit to end.

Change to 3.5mm straight needles.

Row 3: K3, P4, pm, P4, pm, P10, pm, P4, pm, P3, K3.

Row 4: [Knit to marker, m1r, sm, K1, m1l] 4 times, knit to end. (39 sts)

Row 5: K3, purl to last 3 sts, K3.

Row 6: K2, [K3, P1] to 1 st before marker, [knit to marker, m1r, sm, K1, m1l] twice, K1, [P1, K3] to 2 sts before marker, P1, [knit to marker, m1r, sm, K1, m1l] twice, K1, [P1, K3] to last 2 sts, K2. (47 sts)

Row 7: K3, purl to last 3 sts, K3.

Row 8: [Knit to marker, m1r, sm, K1, m1l] 4 times, knit to end. (55 sts)

Row 9: K3, purl to last 3 sts, K3.

Row 10: [K3, P1] to 1 st before marker, [knit to marker, m1r, sm, K1, m1l] twice, K1, [P1, K3] to 2 sts before marker, P1, [knit to marker, m1r, sm, K1, m1l] twice, K1, [P1, K3] to end. (63 sts)

Rows 11-13: Rpt Rows 7-9. (71 sts)

Row 14 (buttonhole row): K1, YO, K2tog, [K2, P1, K1] twice, [knit to marker, m1r, sm, K1, m1l] twice, K1, [P1, K3] to 2 sts before marker, P1, [knit to marker, m1r, sm, K1, m1l] twice, K1, [P1, K3] to last 2 sts, K2. (79 sts)

Rows 15-17: Rpt Rows 7-9. (87 sts)

Row 18: As Row 10. (95 sts)

Rows 19-21: Rpt Rows 7-9. (103 sts)

Row 22: As Row 6. (111 sts)

Row 23: Removing markers as you go, K3, P14 (left back), cast off 23 sts purlwise (sleeve), P31 (front), cast off 23 sts purlwise (sleeve), P14, K3 (right back). (65 sts)

Row 24: K17, pm, m1a twice, K31, pm, m1a twice, knit to end. (69 sts)

Row 25: K3, purl to last 3 sts, K3.

Row 26 (buttonhole row): K1, YO, K2tog, *[P1, K3] to 2 sts before marker, P1, K4; rpt from * once more, [P1, K3] to end.

Row 27: K3, purl to last 3 sts, K3.

Row 28: [Knit to marker, m1r, sm, K2, m1l] twice, knit to end. (73 sts)

Row 29: K3, purl to last 3 sts, K3.

Row 30: K2, [K3, P1] to marker, K2, [P1, K3] to 1 st before marker, P1, K2, [P1, K3] to last 2 sts, K2.

Rows 31-33: Rpt Rows 27-29. (77 sts)

Row 34: [K3, P1] to 3 sts before marker, K4, [P1, K3] to marker, P1, K4, [P1, K3] to end.

Rows 35-37: Rpt Rows 27-29. (81 sts)

Row 38 (buttonhole row): K1, YO, K2tog, K2, *[P1, K3] to 3 sts before marker, P1, K2; rpt from * once more, [P1, K3] to last 2 sts, K2.

Row 39: K3, purl to last 3 sts, K3.

Row 40: Knit.

Row 41: K3, purl to last 3 sts, K3.

Row 42: K3, [P3, m1l, K1, m1r] to last 6 sts, P3, K3. (117 sts)

Row 43: K3, [K3, P3] to last 6 sts, K6.

Row 44: K3, [P3, m1l, K3, m1r] to last 6 sts, P3, K3. (153 sts)

Row 45: K3, [K3, P5] to last 6 sts, K6.

Row 46: K3, [P3, m1l, K5, m1r] to last 6 sts, P3, K3. (189 sts)

Row 47: K3, [K3, P7] to last 6 sts, K6.

Row 48: K3, [P3, K7] to last 6 sts, P3, K3.

Row 49: Knit.

Cast-off row: Rpt Row 48, casting off all sts as you work them.

MAKING UP

1. Block tunic.

2. Sew buttons in place on left-hand button band, down back of tunic, matching them up with the buttonholes.

CAPRI PANTS

The pants are worked top down with no seams except for the frills, which are made separately and sewn on afterwards. The top part is worked back and forth with a button band down the back and some short row shaping for the bottom. The lower half and legs are worked in the round.

Using Yarn B and 3mm straight needles, cast on 52 sts.

Row 1 (ws): Knit.

Row 2: Knit.

Row 3 (buttonhole row): Knit to last 3 sts, K2tog, YO, K1.

Rows 4-5: Knit 2 rows.

Change to 3.5mm straight needles.

Row 6: [K1, K1fb] 11 times, K1fb 3 times, K1, K1fb 4 times, [K1, K1fb] 10 times, K2. (80 sts)

Row 7: K2, P8, turn.

Row 8: YO, knit to end.

Row 9: K2, P8, SSP, P2, turn.

Row 10: YO, knit to end.

Row 11: K2, P11, SSP, P2, turn.

Row 12: YO, knit to end.

Row 13: K2, P14, SSP, P2, turn.

Row 14: YO, knit to end.

Row 15: K2, P17, SSP, purl to last 2 sts, K2.

Row 16: K10, turn.

Row 17: YO, purl to last 2 sts, K2.

Row 18: K10, K2tog, K2, turn.

Row 19 (buttonhole row): YO, purl to last 3 sts, P2tog, YO, K1.

Row 20: K13, K2tog, K2, turn.

Row 21: YO, purl to last 2 sts, K2.

Row 22: K16, K2tog, K2, turn.

Row 23: YO, purl to last 2 sts, K2.

Row 24: K19, K2tog, knit to end.

Row 25: K2, purl to last 2 sts, K2.

Row 26: Knit.

Row 27 (buttonhole row): K2, purl to last 3 sts, P2tog, YO, K1.

Row 28: Knit.

Row 29: K2, purl to last 2 sts, K2.

Rows 30-31: Rpt last 2 rows once more.

Row 32: Transfer sts to a 3.5mm circular needle and knit to last 2 sts, slip the last 2 sts (without working them) onto a cable needle.

Join to work in the round:

Rnd 33: Position the cable needle behind the first 2 sts on the left-hand needle, knit first st on left-hand needle together with first st on cable needle, place marker for beginning of round, knit next st on left-hand needle together with remaining st on cable needle, knit to end. (78 sts)

Rnds 34-37: Knit 4 rnds.

Rnd 38: K1, m1l, knit to last st, m1r, K1. (80 sts)

Rnds 39-40: Knit 2 rnds.

Rnd 41: K1, m1l, knit to last st, m1r, K1. (82 sts)

Rnd 42: K40, m1r, K2, m1l, knit to end. (84 sts)

Rnd 43: K1, m1l, knit to last st, m1r, K1. (86 sts)

Rnd 44: Knit.

Rnd 45: K1, m1l, K41, m1r, K2, m1l, K41, m1r, K1. (90 sts)

Rnd 46: Knit.

Rnd 47: K1, m1l, K43, m1r, K2, m1l, K43, m1r, K1. (94 sts)

Rnd 48: Knit.

Divide for legs:

Rnd 49: K47 (right leg), place next 47 sts (without working them) onto waste yarn (left leg).

RIGHT LEG

Rnds 50-53: Knit 4 rnds.

Rnd 54: SSK, K22, K2tog, knit to end. (45 sts)

Rnds 55-61: Knit 7 rnds.

Rnd 62: SSK, K20, K2tog, knit to end. (43 sts)

Rnds 63-67: Knit 5 rnds.

Rnd 68: SSK, K18, K2tog, knit to end. (41 sts)

Rnd 69: K19, P1, K3, P1, knit to end.

Rnds 70-73: Rpt last rnd 4 more times.

Rnd 74: SSK, K15, K2tog, P1, K3, P1, knit to end. (39 sts)

Rnd 75: K17, P1, K3, P1, knit to end.

Rnds 76-79: Rpt last rnd 4 more times.

Change to 3mm circular needle.

Rnd 80: Knit.

Rnd 81: Purl.

Rnd 82: [K2, K2tog] to last 3 sts, K3. (30 sts)

Rnd 83: Purl.

Picot cast-off: K2, pass bottom st on right-hand needle over top st (photo 1), *slip this st back onto left-hand needle, cast on 2 sts (photo 2), cast off 4 sts (photo 3); rpt from * until all sts have been cast off.

LEFT LEG

Rnd 49: Transfer sts from waste yarn onto 3.5mm circular needle, rejoin yarn and knit 1 rnd, placing marker for beginning of rnd.

Rnds 50-53: Knit 4 rnds.

Rnd 54: K21, SSK, K22, K2tog. (45 sts)

Rnds 55-61: Knit 7 rnds.

Rnd 62: K21, SSK, K20, K2tog. (43 sts)

Rnds 63-67: Knit 5 rnds.

Rnd 68: K21, SSK, K18, K2tog. (41 sts)

Rnd 69: K17, P1, K3, P1, knit to end.

Rnds 70-73: Rpt last rnd 4 more times.

Rnd 74: K17, P1, K3, P1, SSK, K15, K2tog. (39 sts)

Rnd 75: K17, P1, K3, P1, knit to end.

Rnds 76-79: Rpt last rnd 4 more times.

Change to 3mm circular needle.

Rnd 80: Knit.

Rnd 81: Purl.

Rnd 82: K1, [K2, K2tog] to last 2 sts, K2. (30 sts)

Rnd 83: Purl.

Picot cast-off: K2, pass bottom st on right-hand needle over top st, *slip this st back onto left-hand needle, cast on 2 sts, cast off 4 sts; rpt from * until all sts have been cast off.

FRILL (MAKE 4)

Using Yarn A and 3.5mm straight needles, cast on 11 sts.

Row 1 (ws): [K1, P1] to last st, K1.

Cast-off row: K1, [K1, P1] to last 2 sts, K2 (casting off all sts as you work them).

MAKING UP

1. If necessary, close hole with a couple of stitches where the 2 legs join.

2. Block pants.

3. With right side of frills facing you, sew in place along the groove created by the vertical line of purl stitches at the bottom of each leg.

4. Sew 3 buttons in place at the bottom of each leg, between the 2 frills.

5. Sew buttons in place on left-hand button band down back of pants, matching them up with the buttonholes.

SHRUG

The shrug is worked top down, seamlessly and with raglan sleeves. The shrug is worked back and forth in rows and the sleeves are worked in the round.

Using Yarn C and 3mm straight needles, cast on 39 sts.

Row 1 (ws): Knit.

Row 2 (buttonhole row): K1, YO, K2tog, knit to end.

Change to 3.5mm straight needles.

Row 3: K3, P5, pm, P6, pm, P12, pm, P6, pm, P4, K3.

Row 4: [Knit to marker, m1r, sm, K1, m1l] 4 times, knit to end. (47 sts)

Row 5: K3, purl to last 3 sts, K3.

Rows 6-11: Rpt last 2 rows 3 more times. (71 sts)

Row 12: K3, SSK, [knit to marker, m1r, sm, K1, m1l] 4 times, knit to last 5 sts, K2tog, K3. (77 sts)

Row 13: K3, purl to last 3 sts, K3.

Row 14: [Knit to marker, m1r, sm, K1, m1l] 4 times, knit to end. (85 sts)

Row 15: K3, purl to last 3 sts, K3.

Rows 16-19: Rpt Rows 12-15. (99 sts)

Rows 20-23: Rpt Rows 12-13 twice. (111 sts)

Row 24: K3, SSK, *knit to marker, sm, K1 (left front), place next 25 sts (without working them) onto waste yarn (sleeve), remove marker; rpt from * once more (back and second sleeve), knit to last 5 sts, K2tog, K3 (right front). (59 sts)

Row 25: K3, purl to last 3 sts, K3.

Row 26: K3, SSK, [knit to marker, m1r, sm, K2, m1l] twice, knit to last 5 sts, K2tog, K3. (61 sts)

Row 27: K3, purl to last 3 sts, K3.

Row 28: K3, SSK, knit to last 5 sts, K2tog, K3. (59 sts)

Row 29: K3, P2tog, purl to last 5 sts, SSP, K3. (57 sts)

Rows 30-32: Rpt last 2 rows once more, then rpt Row 28 again. (51 sts)

Change to 3mm straight needles.

Rows 33-35: Knit 3 rows.

Picot cast off: K2, pass first st on right-hand needle over 2nd, *slip st back onto left-hand needle, cast on 2 sts, cast off 4 sts; rpt from * until all stitches have been cast off.

SLEEVES

Starting at under arm, slip the 25 sts held on waste yarn for one sleeve evenly onto three 3.5mm dpns and rejoin yarn. Using fourth dpn, start knitting in the round.

Rnds 1-3: Knit 3 rnds.

Rnd 4: K1, m1l, knit to last st, m1r, K1. (27 sts)

Rnds 5-11: Knit 7 rnds.

Rnd 12: K1, m1l, knit to last st, m1r, K1. (29 sts)

Rnds 13-18: Knit 6 rnds.

Change to a set of 3mm dpns.

Rnd 19: Knit.

Rnd 20: Purl.

Rnd 21: [K2, K2tog] to last st, K1. (22 sts)

Rnd 22: Purl.

Picot cast-off: K2, pass first st on right-hand needle over 2nd, *slip st back onto left-hand needle, cast on 2 sts, cast off 4 sts; rpt from * until all stitches have been cast off.

Rpt for second sleeve.

MAKING UP

1. Block shrug.

2. Sew button in place at the top of right-hand button band, matching it up with the buttonhole.

MARY JANE SHOES

Using Yarn B for the soles and changing to Yarn C for the upper parts of the shoes, follow the pattern for the Mary Jane Shoes (see Shoes and Accessories).

CHARLOTTE
THE FOX

What a smart fox Charlotte is, in every sense!
Her pretty dress and linen coat are the perfect
ensemble for a trip to the city. She's off to the science
museum with her packed lunch in her satchel.

YOU WILL NEED

FOR CHARLOTTE'S BODY
• Scheepjes Stonewashed (50g/130m; 78% cotton/ 22% acrylic) yarn in the following shades:

   - *Yarn A* Orange (Coral 816), 2 balls

   - *Yarn B* Cream (Moonstone 801), 1 ball

• 2.75mm (US 2) straight needles

• Toy stuffing

• 2 x 10mm (½in) buttons

• Scrap piece of 4-ply yarn for embroidering nose

FOR CHARLOTTE'S OUTFIT
• Scheepjes Catona (10g/25m, 25g/62m or 50g/125m; 100% cotton) yarn in the following shades:

   - *Yarn A* Green (Sage Green 212), 2 x 50g balls

   - *Yarn B* Pale Blue (Baby Blue 509), 1 x 50g ball

   - *Yarn C* Cream (Old Lace 130), 1 x 25g ball

   - *Yarn D* Brown (Root Beer 157), 1 x 10g ball

• 3.5mm (US 4) straight needles

• 3.5mm (US 4) circular needle (23cm/9in length)

• Set of four 3.5mm (US 4) double-pointed needles

• 3mm (US 2½) straight needles

• 3mm (US 2½) circular needle (23cm/9in length)

• Set of four 3mm (US 2½) double-pointed needles

• Waste yarn

• Cable needle

• Stitch holder

• 14 small buttons

Before you start, please read the Essential Notes at the beginning of this book.

FOX PATTERN

HEAD

Starting at neck:

Using Yarn A and 2.75mm straight needles, cast on 11 sts.

Row 1 (ws): (A) P4, (B) P3, (A) P4.

Row 2: (A) [K1, M1] 3 times, K1, (B) [M1, K1] 3 times, M1, (A) [K1, M1] 3 times, K1. (21 sts)

Row 3: (A) P7, (B) P7, (A) P7.

Row 4: (A) [K2, M1] 3 times, K1, (B) K1, M1, [K2, M1] 3 times, (A) [K2, M1] 3 times, K1. (31 sts)

Row 5: (A) P10, (B) P11, (A) P10.

Row 6: (A) K1, m1l, K9, (B) K11, (A) K9, m1r, K1. (33 sts)

Row 7: (A) P11, (B) P11, (A) P11.

Row 8: (A) K1, m1l, K10, (B) K5, m1r, K1, m1l, K5, (A) K10, m1r, K1. (37 sts)

Row 9: (A) P12, (B) P13, (A) P12.

Row 10: (A) K1, m1l, K11, (B) K6, m1r, K1, m1l, K6, (A) K11, m1r, K1. (41 sts)

Row 11: (A) P13, (B) P7, m1pl, P1, m1pr, P7, (A) P13. (43 sts)

Row 12: (A) K1, m1l, K12, (B) K8, m1r, K1, m1l, K8, (A) K12, m1r, K1. (47 sts)

Row 13: (A) P14, (B) P9, m1pl, P1, m1pr, P9, (A) P14. (49 sts)

Row 14: (A) K14, (B) K10, m1r, K1, m1l, K10, (A) K14. (51 sts)

Row 15: (A) P14, (B) P11, m1pl, P1, m1pr, P11, (A) P14. (53 sts)

Row 16: (A) K1, m1l, K13, (B) K12, m1r, K1, m1l, K12, (A) K13, m1r, K1. (57 sts)

Row 17: (A) P15, (B) P27, (A) P15.

Row 18: (A) K15, (B) K13, m1r, K1, m1l, K13, (A) K15. (59 sts)

Row 19: (A) P15, (B) P29, (A) P15.

Row 20: (A) K16, (B) K13, sl1, K13, (A) K16.

Row 21: (A) P16, (B) P27, (A) P16.

Row 22: (A) K17, (B) K11, CDD, K11, (A) K17. (57 sts)

Continue in Yarn A only.

Row 23: Purl.

Row 24: K27, CDD, K27. (55 sts)

Row 25: P26, PCDD, P26. (53 sts)

Row 26: K25, CDD, K25. (51 sts)

Row 27: P24, PCDD, P24. (49 sts)

Row 28: K1, K2tog, K20, CDD, K20, SSK, K1. (45 sts)

Row 29: P21, PCDD, P21. (43 sts)

Row 30: K20, CDD, K20. (41 sts)

Row 31: Purl.

Row 32: K1, K2tog, K17, sl1, K17, SSK, K1. (39 sts)

Row 33: Purl.

Row 34: K19, sl1, K19.

Row 35: Purl.

Row 36: K1, K2tog, K16, sl1, K16, SSK, K1. (37 sts)

Row 37: Purl.

Row 38: K18, sl1, K18.

Row 39: Purl.

Row 40: K1, K2tog, K3, K2tog 4 times, K3, CDD, K3, SSK 4 times, K3, SSK, K1. (25 sts)

Row 41: Purl.

Row 42: K1, K2tog 5 times, CDD, SSK 5 times, K1. (13 sts)

Row 43: Purl.

Cast off.

EARS (MAKE 2)

Using Yarn A and 2.75mm straight needles, cast on 21 sts.

Row 1 (ws): (A) P8, (B) P5, (A) P8.

Row 2: (A) K8, (B) [K1, M1] 4 times, K1, (A) K8. (25 sts)

Row 3: (A) P8, (B) P9, (A) P8.

Row 4: (A) K8, (B) K9, (A) K8.

Rows 5-7: Rpt last 2 rows once more, then rpt Row 3 again.

Row 8: (A) K5, K2tog, K1, (B) SSK, K5, K2tog, (A) K1, SSK, K5. (21 sts)

Row 9: (A) P7, (B) P7, (A) P7.

Row 10: (A) K7, (B) K7, (A) K7.

Row 11: (A) P7, (B) P7, (A) P7.

Row 12: (A) K4, K2tog, K1, (B) SSK, K3, K2tog, (A) K1, SSK, K4. (17 sts)

Row 13: (A) P6, (B) P5, (A) P6.

Row 14: (A) K3, K2tog, K1, (B) SSK, K1, K2tog, (A) K1, SSK, K3. (13 sts)

Row 15: (A) P5, (B) P3, (A) P5.

Continue in Yarn A only.

Row 16: K2, K2tog, SSK, K1, K2tog, SSK, K2. (9 sts)

Row 17: Purl.

Row 18: K1, K2tog, sl1 kw, K2tog, PSSO, SSK, K1. (5 sts)

Row 19: Purl.

Cut yarn leaving a long tail. Using a tapestry needle, thread tail through the stitches left on needle and pull up tight to gather stitches.

TAIL

Using Yarn A and 2.75mm straight needles, cast on 19 sts.

Row 1 (ws): Purl.

Rows 2-5: Stocking stitch 4 rows.

Row 6: K4, [M1, K6] twice, M1, K3. (22 sts)

Rows 7-9: Stocking stitch 3 rows.

Row 10: K1, [M1, K7] 3 times. (25 sts)

Rows 11-13: Stocking stitch 3 rows.

Row 14: K3, [M1, K4] 5 times, M1, K2. (31 sts)

Rows 15-36: Stocking stitch 22 rows.

Change to Yarn B.

Row 37: Purl.

Row 38: K6, SSK, K1, K2tog, K20. (29 sts)

Row 39: Purl.

Row 40: K19, SSK, K1, K2tog, K5. (27 sts)

Row 41: Purl.

Row 42: K5, SSK, K1, K2tog, K17. (25 sts)

Row 43: Purl.

Row 44: [K4, SSK, K1, K2tog, K3] twice, K1. (21 sts)

Row 45: Purl.

Row 46: [K3, SSK, K1, K2tog, K2] twice, K1. (17 sts)

Row 47: Purl.

Row 48: [K2, SSK, K1, K2tog, K1] twice, K1. (13 sts)

Row 49: Purl.

Row 50: [K1, SSK, K1, K2tog] twice, K1. (9 sts)

Row 51: Purl.

Row 52: SSK, K1, K2tog, CDD, K1. (5 sts)

Rows 53-54: Stocking stitch 2 rows.

Cut yarn leaving a long tail. Using a tapestry needle, thread tail through the stitches left on needle and pull up tight to gather stitches.

BODY

Work as Standard Body – Contrast Front (see Standard Body Parts).

ARMS (MAKE 2)

Work as Standard Arms (see Standard Body Parts).

LEGS (MAKE 2)

Work as Standard Legs – Contrast Foot Pad (see Standard Body Parts).

MAKING UP

Follow the instructions in the techniques section (see Techniques: Making Up Your Animal).

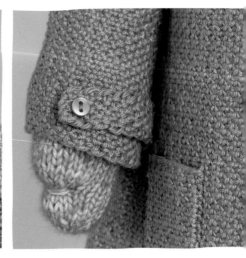

OUTFIT PATTERNS

LINEN STITCH COAT

The coat is worked top down, with raglan sleeves and no seams except for the pockets, which are made separately and sewn on afterwards. The coat, collar and pockets are worked back and forth in rows and the sleeves are worked in the round.

Using Yarn A and 3.5mm straight needles, cast on 55 sts.

Row 1 (ws): K1, [P1, sl1wyib] 4 times, P2, pm, [P1, sl1wyib] 3 times, P2, pm, [P1, sl1wyib] 8 times, P2, pm, [P1, sl1wyib] 3 times, P2, pm, [P1, sl1wyib] to last 2 sts, P1, K1.

Row 2: [K1, sl1wyif] to marker, m1r, sm, K1, m1l, *[sl1wyif, K1] to 1 st before marker, sl1wyif, m1r, sm, K1, m1l; rpt from * twice more, [sl1wyif, K1] to end. (63 sts)

Row 3: K1, [P1, sl1wyib] to last 2 sts, P1, K1.

Row 4 (buttonhole row): K1, sl1wyif, YO, SSK, [sl1wyif, K1] to marker, m1r, sm, K1, m1l, *[K1, sl1wyif] to 1 st before marker, K1, m1r, sm, K1, m1l; rpt from * twice more, K1, [sl1wyif, K1] to end. (71 sts)

Row 5: K1, *[P1, sl1wyib] to 2 sts before marker, P2, sm; rpt from * 3 more times, [P1, sl1wyib] to last 2 sts, P1, K1.

Row 6: [K1, sl1wyif] to marker, m1r, sm, K1, m1l, *[sl1wyif, K1] to 1 st before marker, sl1wyif, m1r, sm, K1, m1l; rpt from * twice more, [sl1wyif, K1] to end. (79 sts)

Row 7: K1, [P1, sl1wyib] to last 2 sts, P1, K1.

Row 8: *[K1, sl1wyif] to 1 st before marker, K1, m1r, sm, K1, m1l; rpt from * 3 more times, [K1, sl1wyif] to last st, K1. (87 sts)

Rows 9-19: Rpt Rows 5-8 twice more, then rpt Rows 5-7 again. (127 sts)

Row 20 (buttonhole row): As Row 4. (135 sts)

Rows 21-33: Rpt Rows 5-8 3 times, then rpt Row 5 again. (183 sts)

Row 34: [K1, sl1wyif] to marker, remove marker, K1 (left front), place next 39 sts (without working them) onto waste yarn (sleeve), sm, m1a, [K1, sl1wyif] to marker, remove marker, K1 (back), place next 39 sts (without working them) onto waste yarn (sleeve), sm, m1a, [K1, sl1wyif] to last st, K1 (right front). (107 sts)

Row 35: K1, [P1, sl1wyib] to last 2 sts, P1, K1.

Row 36 (buttonhole row): K1, sl1wyif, YO, SSK, [sl1wyif, K1] to last st, K1.

Row 37: K1, [P1, sl1wyib] to last 2 sts, P1, K1.

Row 38: [K1, sl1wyif] to last st, K1.

Row 39: K1, [P1, sl1wyib] to last 2 sts, P1, K1.

Row 40: *[K1, sl1wyif] to 1 st before marker, K1, m1r, sm, K1, m1l; rpt from * once more, [K1, sl1wyif] to last st, K1. (111 sts)

Rows 41-43: Rpt Rows 37-39.

The left and right sides of the coat are now worked separately, creating an overlapping vent down the centre back.

LEFT SIDE

Row 44: [K1, sl1wyif] 28 times, K1, place next 54 sts (without working them) onto a stitch holder. (57 sts)

Row 45: K1, [P1, sl1wyib] to last 2 sts, P1, K1.

Row 46: [K1, sl1wyif] to last st, K1.

Rows 47-48: Rpt last 2 rows once more.

Row 49: K1, [P1, sl1wyib] to 2 sts before marker, P1, m1pr, sl1wyib, sm, m1pl, [P1, sl1wyib] to last 2 sts, P1, K1. (59 sts)

Rows 50-51: Rpt Rows 38-39.

Row 52 (buttonhole row): Work as Row 36 of Coat.

Rows 53-57: Rpt Rows 37-38 of Coat twice, then rpt Row 37 of Coat again.

Row 58: [K1, sl1wyif] to 1 st before marker, K1, m1r, sm, sl1wyif, m1l, [K1, sl1wyif] to last st, K1. (61 sts)

Rows 59-66: Rpt Rows 37-38 of Coat 4 times.

Row 67: K1, [P1, sl1wyib] to 2 sts before marker, P1, m1pr, sl1wyib, sm, m1pl, [P1, sl1wyib] to last 2 sts, P1, K1. (63 sts)

Rows 68-75: Rpt Rows 38-39 of Coat 4 times.

Row 76: [K1, sl1wyif] to 1 st before marker, K1, m1r, sm, sl1wyif, m1l, [K1, sl1wyif] to last st, K1. (65 sts)

Rows 77-94: Rpt Rows 59-76. (69 sts)

Rows 95-115: Rpt Rows 37-38 of Coat 10 times, then rpt Row 37 of Coat again.

Cast off in pattern.

RIGHT SIDE

Row 44: Transfer the stitches on hold back onto needle. With right side facing you and starting at the centre back, pick up 3 sts from behind the first row of left side (see Techniques: Casting On and Stitches, Picking up stitches), [sl1wyif, K1] to end. (57 sts)

Rows 45-51: Work as Rows 45-51 of Left Side.

Row 52: [K1, sl1wyif] to last st, K1.

Rows 53-115: Work as Rows 53-115 of Left Side.

Cast off in pattern.

SLEEVES

Starting at under arm, slip the 39 sts held on waste yarn for one sleeve evenly onto three 3.5mm dpns and rejoin yarn.

Using fourth dpn, start knitting in the round.

Rnd 1: Pick up and knit 1 st from under arm, [sl1wyif, K1] to last st, sl1wyif, pick up and knit 1 st from under arm. (41 sts)

Rnd 2: [Sl1wyif, K1] to last st, sl1wyif.

Rnd 3: K1, sl1wyif] to last st, K1.

Rnds 4-5: Rpt last 2 rnds once more.

Rnd 6: Sl1wyif, m1l, [K1, sl1wyif] to last 2 sts, K1, m1r, sl1wyif. (43 sts)

Rnd 7: [Sl1wyif, K1] to last st, sl1wyif.

Rnd 8: [K1, sl1wyif] to last st, K1.

Rnds 9-12: Rpt last 2 rnds twice more.

Rnds 13-33: Rpt Rnds 6-12 3 more times. (49 sts)

Rnds 34-36: Rpt Rnds 7-8, then rpt Rnd 7 again.

Cast off in pattern.

Rpt for second sleeve.

COLLAR

Using 3.5mm straight needles, with wrong side of coat facing and beginning and ending 3 sts from centre front edges, pick up and knit 49 sts around neck edge (see Techniques: Casting On and Stitches, Picking up stitches). Right side of collar is on wrong side of coat, so that the right sides are facing out when folded over.

Row 1 (ws): K1, [P1, sl1wyib] to last 2 sts, P1, K1.

Row 2: K1, m1l, [sl1wyif, K1] to last 2 sts, sl1wyif, m1r, K1. (51 sts)

Row 3: K1, P1, [P1, sl1wyib] to last 3 sts, P2, K1.

Row 4: K1, m1l, [K1, sl1wyif] to last 2 sts, K1, m1r, K1. (53 sts)

Rows 5-8: Rpt last 4 rows once more. (57 sts)

Row 9: K1, [P1, sl1wyib] to last 2 sts, P1, K1.

Row 10: [K1, sl1wyif] to last st, K1.

Rows 11-13: Rpt last 2 rows once more, then rpt Row 9 again.

Row 14: [K1, sl1wyif] to last st, sl1wyib.

Row 15: Sl1wyif, P1, PSSO, [sl1wyib, P1] to last st, sl1wyif. (56 sts)

Row 16: Sl1wyib, sl1wyif, pass first st on right-hand needle over second st, [K1, sl1wyif] to last 2 sts, K1, sl1wyib. (55 sts)

Row 17: Sl1wyif, sl1wyib, pass first st on right-hand needle over second st, [P1, sl1wyib] to last st, sl1wyif. (54 sts)

Cast-off row: Sl1wyib, K1, PSSO, sl1wyif, pass bottom st on right-hand needle over top st, *K1, place left-hand needle through front loops of 2 sts on right-hand needle and knit them together through the back loops (photo 1), sl1wyib and knit 2 sts on right-hand needle together through back loops as before; rpt from * until 3 sts remain on left-hand needle, K1, pass

bottom st on right-hand needle over top st, sl1wyif, pass bottom st on right-hand needle over top st, slip st back onto left-hand needle, turn work, pass bottom st over top st.

Cut yarn and fasten off remaining st.

SLEEVE TAB (MAKE 2)

Using Yarn A and 3.5mm straight needles, cast on 17 sts.

Row 1 (ws): K1, [P1, sl1wyib] to last 2 sts, P1, K1.

Row 2: [K1, sl1wyif] to last st, K1.

Rows 3-5: Rpt last 2 rows once more, then rpt Row 1 again.

Cast off in pattern.

POCKET (MAKE 2)

Using Yarn A and 3.5mm straight needles, cast on 15 sts.

Row 1 (ws): K1, [P1, sl1wyib] to last 2 sts, P1, K1.

Row 2: [K1, sl1wyif] to last st, K1.

Rows 3-21: Rpt last 2 rows 9 more times, then rpt Row 1 again.

Cast off in pattern.

MAKING UP

1. Block all pieces.

2. Position sleeve tab on front of sleeve, with short end lined up with centre under arm and approximately 0.5cm (¼in) up from end of sleeve. Sew in place along the bottom short end. Attach button sewing through tab and front of sleeve. Repeat for second sleeve.

3. Position pockets on each front of coat, approximately 2cm (¾in) in from front edge and 4cm (1½in) up from bottom edge. Pin in place. Sew around 3 sides, leaving top of pocket open.

4. Sew buttons in place on right-hand centre front of coat, matching them up with the buttonholes.

DRESS

The dress is worked top down, seamlessly with raglan sleeves. The top half is worked back and forth, with a button band down the back, and the bottom half is worked in the round.

Using Yarn B and 3mm straight needles, cast on 31 sts.

Row 1 (ws): Knit.

Row 2 (buttonhole row): K1, YO, K2tog, knit to end.

Row 3: Knit.

Row 4: K3, [K1, K1fb] to last 4 sts, K4. (43 sts)

Rows 5-7: Knit 3 rows.

Row 8: K3, [K2, K1fb] to last 4 sts, K4. (55 sts)

Change to 3.5mm straight needles.

Row 9: K3, P7, pm, P10, pm, P16, pm, P10, pm, P6, K3.

Row 10: *[Knit to marker, m1r, sm, K1, m1l] twice*, K2, [YO, K3, pass 1st of the 3 knit sts over the 2nd and 3rd] 4 times, rpt from * to *, knit to end. (63 sts)

Row 11: K3, purl to last 3 sts, K3.

Row 12: *[Knit to marker, m1r, sm, K1, m1l] twice*, K2, [K3, pass 1st of the 3 knit sts over the 2nd and 3rd, YO] 4 times, rpt from * to *, knit to end. (71 sts)

Row 13: K3, purl to last 3 sts, K3.

Row 14: *[Knit to marker, m1r, sm, K1, m1l] twice*, K4, [YO, K3, pass 1st of the 3 knit sts over the 2nd and 3rd] 4 times, rpt from * to *, knit to end. (79 sts)

Row 15: K3, purl to last 3 sts, K3.

Row 16 (buttonhole row): K1, YO, K2tog, *[knit to marker, m1r, sm, K1, m1l] twice*, K4, [K3, pass 1st of the 3 knit sts over the 2nd and 3rd, YO] 4 times, rpt from * to *, knit to end. (87 sts)

Row 17: K3, purl to last 3 sts, K3.

Row 18: *[Knit to marker, m1r, sm, K1, m1l] twice*, K6, [YO, K3, pass 1st of the 3 knit sts over the 2nd and 3rd] 4 times, rpt from * to *, knit to end. (95 sts)

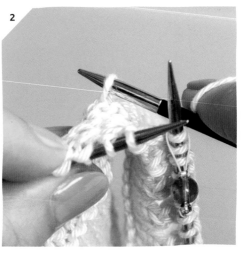

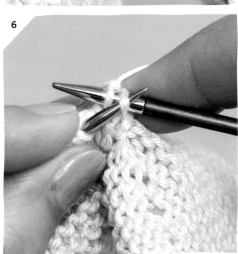

Row 19: K3, purl to last 3 sts, K3.

Row 20: *[Knit to marker, m1r, sm, K1, m1l] twice*, K6, [K3, pass 1st of the 3 knit sts over the 2nd and 3rd, YO] 4 times, rpt from * to *, knit to end. (103 sts)

Row 21: K3, purl to last 3 sts, K3.

Row 22: *[Knit to marker, m1r, sm, K1, m1l] twice*, K8, [YO, K3, pass 1st of the 3 knit sts over the 2nd and 3rd] 4 times, rpt from * to *, knit to end. (111 sts)

Row 23: K3, purl to last 3 sts, K3.

Row 24: *[Knit to marker, m1r, sm, K1, m1l] twice*, K8, [K3, pass 1st of the 3 knit sts over the 2nd and 3rd, YO] 4 times, rpt from * to *, knit to end. (119 sts)

Row 25: K3, *purl to marker (remove marker), cast off next 25 sts, sm; rpt from * once more, purl to last 3 sts, K3. (69 sts)

Row 26: K29, [YO, K3, pass 1st of the 3 knit sts over the 2nd and 3rd] 4 times, knit to end.

Row 27: K3, purl to last 3 sts, K3.

Row 28: *Knit to marker, m1r, sm, K2, m1l*, K10, P11, rpt from * to *, knit to end. (73 sts)

Row 29: K3, purl to last 3 sts, K3.

Row 30 (buttonhole row): K1, YO, K2tog, K28, P11, knit to end.

Row 31: K3, purl to last 3 sts, K3.

Row 32: K31, P11, knit to end.

Row 33: K3, purl to last 3 sts, K3.

Row 34: *Knit to marker, m1r, sm, K2, m1l*, K11, m1r, K3, m1r, K2, m1r, K1, m1l, K2, m1l, K3, m1l, rpt from * to *, knit to end. (83 sts)

Row 35: K3, purl to last 3 sts, K3.

Row 36: Knit.

Rows 37-39: Rpt last 2 rows once more, then rpt Row 35 again.

Row 40: [Knit to marker, m1r, sm, K2, m1l] twice, knit to end. (87 sts)

Row 41: K3, purl to last 3 sts, K3.

Row 42 (buttonhole row): K1, YO, K2tog, knit to end.

Rows 43-45: Rpt Rows 35-36 once more, then rpt Row 35 again.

Row 46: As Row 40. (91 sts)

Rows 47-51: Rpt Rows 35-36 twice, then rpt Row 35 again.

Row 52: As Row 40. (95 sts)

Row 53: K3, P to last 3 sts, K3.

Row 54: Transfer sts to a 3.5mm circular needle, knit to last 3 sts, slip the last 3 sts (without working them) onto a cable needle.

Join to work in the round:

Rnd 55: Position cable needle behind first 3 sts on left-hand needle, place marker for beginning of round, knit first st on left-hand needle together with first st on cable needle, rpt for next 2 sts, knit to end. (92 sts)

Rnd 56-57: Knit 2 rnds.

Rnd 58: [Knit to marker, m1r, sm, K2, m1l] twice, knit to end. (96 sts)

Rnds 59-65: Knit 7 rnds.

Rnd 66: As Rnd 58. (100 sts)

Rnds 67-74: Knit 8 rnds.

Rnd 75: Purl.

Rnd 76: Knit.

Rnds 77-80: Rpt last 2 rnds twice more.

Rnds 81-83: Knit 3 rnds.

Rnd 84: [YO, K2tog] to end.

Change to a 3mm circular needle.

Rnds 85-87: Knit 3 rnds.

Hemmed picot cast-off: Using a larger needle so cast off is looser, pick up the purl bump 8 rnds down (photo 2) (this will be the first 'u' purl bump before the garter stitch row) and place it onto the left-hand needle (photo 3), then knit it together with the next stitch (photo 4). Pick up the next purl bump 8 rnds down and knit together with the next st, you now have 2 sts on the right-hand needle (photo 5), pass the bottom stitch over the top stitch to cast off (photo 6). Rpt until all sts have been cast off.

MAKING UP

1. Block dress.

2. Sew buttons in place on left-hand button band down back of dress, matching them up with the buttonholes.

MESSENGER BAG

The bag is worked in one piece and seamed at either side, with an i-cord strap.

Using Yarn D and 3mm straight needles, cast on 17 sts.

Row 1 (ws): Knit.

Rows 2-37: Stocking stitch 36 rows.

Row 38: Knit.

Row 39: K2, purl to last 2 sts, K2.

Rows 40-45: Rpt last 2 rows 3 more times.

Row 46: K2, SSK, knit to last 4 sts, K2tog, K2. (15 sts)

Row 47: K2, P2tog, purl to last 4 sts, SSP, K2. (13 sts)

Rows 48-49: Rpt last 2 rows once more. (9 sts)

Row 50 (buttonhole row): K2, sl1, K2tog, PSSO, YO, K2tog, K2. (7 sts)

Row 51: K1, K2tog, P1, SSK, K1. (5 sts)

Row 52: K1, sl1, K2tog, PSSO, K1. (3 sts)

Row 53: Knit.

Cut yarn leaving a long tail. Using a tapestry needle, thread tail through the stitches left on needle and pull up tight to gather stitches.

STRAP

Using Yarn D and two 3.5mm dpns, cast on 4 sts.

Make an i-cord of 85 rows, approximately 24cm (9½in), see Techniques: Casting On and Stitches, Making i-cord).

MAKING UP

1. Block bag.

2. Fold the bag in half with the right side on the outside, lining up the cast-on edge just below the start of the garter edging on the bag flap. Sew up both side seams.

3. Fold over the bag flap and press lightly.

4. Sew a button in place on centre front of bag, matching it up with the buttonhole.

5. Sew an end of the strap to the top of each side seam.

FRENCH KNICKERS

Using Yarn C, follow the pattern for the French Knickers (see Shoes and Accessories).

ARCHIE
THE SQUIRREL

Lucky for Archie that he's good with a spreadsheet, or he'd never keep track of where he hid last year's nuts. He's just off to check the data now, in his tie and waistcoat, summer shorts and T-bar shoes.

YOU WILL NEED

FOR ARCHIE'S BODY

- Scheepjes Stonewashed (50g/130m; 78% cotton/22% acrylic) yarn in the following shades:

  - *Yarn A* Orange (Coral 816), 2 balls

  - *Yarn B* Cream (Moonstone 801), 1 ball

- 2.75mm (US 2) straight needles

- Toy stuffing

- 2 x 10mm (½in) buttons

- Scrap piece of 4-ply yarn for embroidering nose

FOR ARCHIE'S OUTFIT

- Scheepjes Catona (10g/25m, 25g/62m or 50g/125m; 100% cotton) yarn in the following shades:

  - *Yarn A* Cream (Old Lace 130), 1 x 50g ball

  - *Yarn B* Dark Blue (Light Navy 164), 1 x 50g ball

  - *Yarn C* Green (Sage Green 212), 1 x 50g ball

- 2.75mm (US 2) straight needles

- 3mm (US 2½) straight needles

- 3mm (US 2½) circular needle (23cm/9in length)

- Set of four 3mm (US 2½) double-pointed needles

- 3.5mm (US 4) straight needles

- 3.5mm (US 4) circular needle (23cm/9in length)

- Set of four 3.5mm (US 4) double-pointed needles

- Cable needle

- Waste yarn

- 11 small buttons

Before you start, please read the Essential Notes at the beginning of this book.

SQUIRREL PATTERN

HEAD

Starting at neck:

Using Yarn A and 2.75mm straight needles, cast on 11 sts.

Row 1 (ws): Purl.

Row 2: [K1, M1] to last st, K1. (21 sts)

Row 3: Purl.

Row 4: [K2, M1] to last st, K1. (31 sts)

Row 5: Purl.

Row 6: K1, m1l, knit to last st, m1r, K1. (33 sts)

Row 7: Purl.

Row 8: [K1, m1l, K15, m1r] twice, K1. (37 sts)

Row 9: Purl.

Row 10: [K1, m1l, K17, m1r] twice, K1. (41 sts)

Row 11: P20, m1pl, P1, m1pr, P20. (43 sts)

Row 12: (A) K1, m1l, K20, m1r, (B) K1, (A) m1l, K20, m1r, K1. (47 sts)

Row 13: (A) P23, (B) m1pl, P1, m1pr, (A) P23. (49 sts)

Row 14: (A) K22, (B) K2, m1r, K1, m1l, K2, (A) K22. (51 sts)

Row 15: (A) P21, (B) P9, (A) P21.

Row 16: (A) K1, m1l, K20, (B) K4, m1r, K1, m1l, K4, (A) K20, m1r, K1. (55 sts)

Row 17: (A) P22, (B) P11, (A) P22.

Row 18: (A) K22, (B) K5, sl1, K5, (A) K22.

Row 19: (A) P22, (B) P11, (A) P22.

Row 20: (A) K23, (B) K4, sl1, K4, (A) K23.

Continue in Yarn A only.

Row 21: Purl.

Row 22: K26, CDD, K26. (53 sts)

Row 23: Purl.

Row 24: K25, CDD, K25. (51 sts)

Row 25: Purl.

Row 26: K24, CDD, K24. (49 sts)

Row 27: Purl.

Row 28: K1, K2tog, K20, CDD, K20, SSK, K1. (45 sts)

Row 29: Purl.

Row 30: K21, CDD, K21. (43 sts)

Row 31: Purl.

Row 32: K1, K2tog, K17, CDD, K17, SSK, K1. (39 sts)

Row 33: Purl.

Row 34: K19, sl1, K19.

Row 35: Purl.

Row 36: K1, K2tog, K16, sl1, K16, SSK, K1. (37 sts)

Row 37: Purl.

Row 38: K18, sl1, K18.

Row 39: Purl.

Row 40: K1, K2tog, K3, K2tog 4 times, K3, CDD, K3, SSK 4 times, K3, SSK, K1. (25 sts)

Row 41: Purl.

Row 42: K1, K2tog 5 times, CDD, SSK 5 times, K1. (13 sts)

Row 43: Purl.

Cast off.

EARS (MAKE 2)

Using Yarn A and 2.75mm straight needles, cast on 14 sts.

Row 1 (ws): Purl.

Row 2: K5, [K1, M1] 3 times, knit to end. (17 sts)

Rows 3–7: Stocking stitch 5 rows.

Row 8: [K3, K2tog, SSK] twice, K3. (13 sts)

Row 9: Purl.

Row 10: K1, [K1, K2tog, SSK] twice, K2. (9 sts)

Row 11: Purl.

Row 12: K1, K2tog, sl1 kw, K2tog, PSSO, SSK, K1. (5 sts)

Row 13: Purl.

Row 14: Knit.

Cut yarn leaving a long tail. Using a tapestry needle, thread tail through the stitches left on needle and pull up tight to gather stitches.

TAIL

Using Yarn A and 2.75mm straight needles, cast on 25 sts.

Row 1 (ws): P3, turn.

Row 2: YO, K3.

Row 3: P3, SSP, P1, turn.

Row 4: YO, K5.

Row 5: P5, SSP, P1, turn.

Row 6: YO, K7.

Row 7: P7, SSP, P1, turn.

Row 8: YO, K9.

Row 9: P9, SSP, P1, turn.

Row 10: YO, K11.

Row 11: P11, SSP, purl to end.

Row 12: K3, turn.

Row 13: YO, P3.

Row 14: K3, K2tog, K1, turn.

Row 15: YO, P5.

Row 16: K5, K2tog, K1, turn.

Row 17: YO, P7.

Row 18: K7, K2tog, K1, turn.

Row 19: YO, P9.

Row 20: K9, K2tog, K1, turn.

Row 21: YO, P11.

Row 22: K11, K2tog, knit to end.

Rows 23–66: Rpt Rows 1–22 twice more.

Rows 67–75: Stocking stitch 9 rows.

Row 76: [K1, m1l, K11, m1r] twice, K1. (29 sts)

Rows 77–87: Stocking stitch 11 rows.

Row 88: [K1, m1l, K13, m1r] twice, K1. (33 sts)

Rows 89–99: Stocking stitch 11 rows.

Row 100: [K1, m1l, K15, m1r] twice, K1. (37 sts)

Row 101: Purl.

Row 102: K35, turn.

Row 103: YO, P33, turn.

Row 104: YO, K31, turn.

Row 105: YO, P29, turn.

Row 106: YO, K27, turn.

Row 107: YO, P25, turn.

Row 108: YO, K23, turn.

Row 109: YO, P21, turn.

Row 110: YO, P19, turn.

Row 111: YO, P17, turn.

Row 112: YO, K15, turn.

Row 113: YO, P13, turn.

Row 114: YO, K13, [K2tog, K1] to end.

Row 115: P25, [SSP, P1] to end.

Rows 116–143: Rpt Rows 102-115 twice more.

Rows 144–145: Stocking stitch 2 rows.

Row 146: K1, K2tog, K31, SSK, K1. (35 sts)

Row 147: Purl.

Row 148: K16, CDD, K16. (33 sts)

Row 149: Purl.

Row 150: K1, K2tog, K27, SSK, K1. (31 sts)

Row 151: Purl.

Row 152: K14, CDD, K14. (29 sts)

Row 153: Purl.

Row 154: K1, K2tog, K10, CDD, K10, SSK, K1. (25 sts)

Row 155: Purl.

Row 156: K11, CDD, K11. (23 sts)

Row 157: Purl.

Row 158: K10, CDD, K10. (21 sts)

Row 159: Purl.

Row 160: K9, CDD, K9. (19 sts)

Row 161: P8, PCDD, P8. (17 sts)

Row 162: K7, CDD, K7. (15 sts)

Row 163: P6, PCDD, P6. (13 sts)

Row 164: K5, CDD, K5. (11 sts)

Row 165: P4, PCDD, P4. (9 sts)

Row 166: K3, CDD, K3. (7 sts)

Row 167: P2, PCDD, P2. (5 sts)

Rows 168–169: Stocking stitch 2 rows.

Cut yarn leaving a long tail. Using a tapestry needle, thread tail through the stitches left on needle and pull up tight to gather stitches.

BODY

Work as Standard Body – Contrast Front (see Standard Body Parts).

ARMS (MAKE 2)

Work as Standard Arms (see Standard Body Parts).

LEGS (MAKE 2)

Work as Standard Legs – Plain (see Standard Body Parts).

MAKING UP

Follow the instructions in the techniques section (see Techniques: Making Up Your Animal).

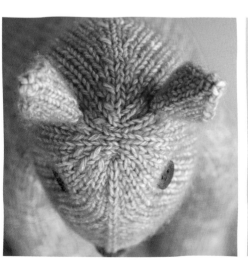

TIE CHART

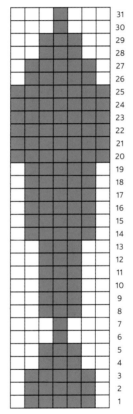

```
31
30
29
28
27
26
25
24
23
22
21
20
19
18
17
16
15
14
13
12
11
10
9
8
7
6
5
4
3
2
1
```

```
7 6 5 4 3 2 1
```

KEY

☐ Yarn A

▨ Yarn B

OUTFIT PATTERNS

TIE T-SHIRT

The T-shirt is worked top down, with raglan sleeves. It is worked back and forth in rows with a button band opening and seam at the back; the sleeves are worked in the round. The tie motif is worked using the Intarsia method (see Techniques: Colourwork)

Using 3mm straight needles and Yarn A, cast on 31 sts.

Row 1 (ws): Knit.

Row 2 (buttonhole row): K1, YO, K2tog, knit to end.

Row 3: Knit.

Row 4: K3, [K1, K1fb, K1] to last 4 sts, K4. (39 sts)

Change to 3.5mm straight needles.

The Tie Chart is worked over the next 31 rows, in stocking stitch and using the Intarsia method (see Techniques: Colourwork). Starting at the bottom left of chart, read WS rows from left to right and RS rows from right to left.

Row 5: K3, P5, pm, P6, pm, P2, work Tie Chart, P3, pm, P6, pm, P4, K3.

Row 6: [Knit to marker, m1r, sm, K1, m1l] twice, K2, work Tie Chart, [knit to marker, m1r, sm, K1, m1l] twice, knit to end. (47 sts)

Row 7: K3, P17, work Tie Chart, purl to last 3 sts, K3.

Row 8: [Knit to marker, m1r, sm, K1, m1l] twice, K3, work Tie Chart, [knit to marker, m1r, sm, K1, m1l] twice, knit to end. (55 sts)

Row 9: K3, P21, work Tie Chart, purl to last 3 sts, K3.

Row 10 (buttonhole row): K1, YO, K2tog, [knit to marker, m1r, sm, K1, m1l] twice, K4, work Tie Chart, [knit to marker, m1r, sm, K1, m1l] twice, knit to end. (63 sts)

Row 11: K3, P25, work Tie Chart, purl to last 3 sts, K3.

Row 12: [Knit to marker, m1r, sm, K1, m1l] twice, K5, work Tie Chart, [knit to marker, m1r, sm, K1, m1l] twice, knit to end. (71 sts)

Row 13: K3, P29, work Tie Chart, purl to last 3 sts, K3.

Row 14: [Knit to marker, m1r, sm, K1, m1l] twice, K6, work Tie Chart, [knit to marker, m1r, sm, K1, m1l] twice, knit to end. (79 sts)

Row 15: K3, P33, work Tie Chart, purl to last 3 sts, K3.

Row 16: [Knit to marker, m1r, sm, K1, m1l] twice, K7, work Tie Chart, [knit to marker, m1r, sm, K1, m1l] twice, knit to end. (87 sts)

Row 17: K3, P37, work Tie Chart, purl to last 3 sts, K3.

Row 18 (buttonhole row): K1, YO, K2tog, [knit to marker, m1r, sm, K1, m1l] twice, K8, work Tie Chart, [knit to marker, m1r, sm, K1, m1l] twice, knit to end. (95 sts)

Row 19: K3, P41, work Tie Chart, purl to last 3 sts, K3.

Row 20: [Knit to marker, m1r, sm, K1, m1l] twice, K9, work Tie Chart, [knit to marker, m1r, sm, K1, m1l] twice, knit to end. (103 sts)

Row 21: K3, P45, work Tie Chart, purl to last 3 sts, K3.

Row 22: [Knit to marker, m1r, sm, K1, m1l] twice, K10, work Tie Chart, [knit to marker, m1r, sm, K1, m1l] twice, knit to end. (111 sts)

Row 23: Cast off 3 sts, P49 (this includes the st from the last cast off), work Tie Chart, purl to last 3 sts, K3. (108 sts)

Row 24: Knit to marker, remove marker, K1, m1a (right back), without working them place next 23 sts onto waste yarn (sleeve), sm, m1a, K12, work Tie Chart, knit to marker, remove marker, K1, m1a (front), without working them place next 23 sts onto waste yarn (sleeve), sm, m1a, knit to end (left back). (66 sts)

Row 25: P28, work Tie Chart, purl to end.

Row 26: Knit to 1 st before marker, m1r, K1, sm, K1, m1l, K12, work Tie Chart, knit to 1 st before marker, m1r, K1, sm, K1, m1l, knit to end. (70 sts)

Row 27: P30, work Tie Chart, purl to end.

Row 28: K33, work Tie Chart, knit to end.

Row 29: As Row 27.

Row 30: Knit to 1 st before marker, m1r, K1, sm, K1, m1l, K13, work Tie Chart, knit to 1 st before marker, m1r, K1, sm, K1, m1l, knit to end. (74 sts)

Row 31: P32, work Tie Chart, purl to end.

Row 32: K35, work Tie Chart, knit to end.

Row 33: As Row 31.

Row 34: Knit to 1 st before marker, m1r, K1, sm, K1, m1l, K14, work Tie Chart, knit to 1 st before marker, m1r, K1, sm, K1, m1l, knit to end. (78 sts)

Row 35: P34, work Tie Chart, purl to end.

Row 36: Knit.

Row 37: Purl.

Change to 3mm straight needles.

Rows 38–41: Knit 4 rows.

Cast off.

SLEEVES

Starting at under arm, slip the 23 sts held on waste yarn for one sleeve evenly onto three 3.5mm dpns and rejoin yarn.

Using fourth dpn, start knitting in the round.

Rnd 1: Pick up and knit 1 stitch from under arm, knit to end, pick up and knit 1 stitch from under arm. (25 sts)

Rnds 2–4: Knit 3 rnds.

Rnd 5: K1, m1l, knit to last st, m1r, K1. (27 sts)

Rnds 6–12: Knit 7 rnds.

Rnd 13: K1, m1l, knit to last st, m1r, K1. (29 sts)

Rnds 14–20: Knit 7 rnds.

Change to a set of 3mm dpns.

Rnd 21: Knit.

Rnd 22: Purl.

Rnds 23-24: Rpt last 2 rnds once more.

Repeat for second sleeve.

MAKING UP

1. If necessary, close hole under arm with a couple of stitches.

2. Block T-shirt.

3. Sew buttons in place on left-hand button band, matching them up with the buttonholes.

WAISTCOAT

The waistcoat is worked in one piece from the bottom up, back and forth in rows and seamed at the shoulders.

Using 3mm straight needles and Yarn C, cast on 100 sts.

Row 1 (ws): Knit.

Rows 2-3: Knit 2 rows.

Change to 3.5mm straight needles.

Row 4 (buttonhole row): K12, CDD, K70, CDD, K9, K2tog, YO, K1. (96 sts)

Row 5: K3, P19, K10, P32, K10, P19, K3.

Row 6: K11, CDD, K68, CDD, K11. (92 sts)

Row 7: K3, P17, K10, P32, K10, P17, K3.

Row 8: K10, CDD, K66, CDD, K10. (88 sts)

Row 9: K3, P15, K5, pm, K5, P32, K5, pm, K5, P15, K3.

Row 10: K9, CDD, [knit to 2 sts before marker, K2tog, sm, SSK] twice, K9, CDD, K9. (80 sts)

Row 11: K3, P3, K7, P3, K8, P32, K8, P3, K7, P3, K3.

Row 12 (buttonhole row): Knit to last 3 sts, K2tog, YO, K1.

Row 13: As Row 11.

Row 14: [Knit to 2 sts before marker, K2tog, sm, SSK] twice, knit to end. (76 sts)

Row 15: K3, P3, K7, P3, K6, P32, K6, P3, K7, P3, K3.

Row 16: Knit.

Row 17: K3, P13, K6, P32, K6, P13, K3.

Row 18: As Row 14. (72 sts)

Row 19: K3, P10, K10, P26, K10, P10, K3.

Row 20 (buttonhole row): K16 (right front), cast off 4 sts, K32 (this includes the st from the last cast off) (back), cast off 4 sts, K13 (this includes the st from the last cast off), K2tog, YO, K1. (64 sts)

The waistcoat is now worked in 3 separate parts.

LEFT FRONT

Worked over the first 16 sts only.

Row 21: K3, P10, K3.

Row 22: K3, SSK, K11. (15 sts)

Row 23: K3, P9, K3.

Row 24: K3, SSK, K5, K2tog, K3. (13 sts)

Row 25: K3, P7, K3.

Row 26: Knit to last 5 sts, K2tog, K3. (12 sts)

Row 27: K3, purl to last 3 sts, K3.

Rows 28–37: Rpt Rows 26–27 5 more times. (7 sts)

Row 38: K2, K2tog, K3. (6 sts)

Row 39: Knit.

Row 40: K1, K2tog, K3. (5 sts)

Rows 41–43: Knit 3 rows.

Cast off.

BACK

With RS facing rejoin yarn and work over the next 32 sts only.

Row 21: K3, purl to last 3 sts, K3.

Row 22: K3, SSK, knit to last 5 sts, K2tog, K3. (30 sts)

Rows 23–24: Rpt Rows 21-22 once more. (28 sts)

Row 25: K3, purl to last 3 sts, K3.

Row 26: Knit.

Rows 27–34: Rpt Rows 25-26 4 more times.

Row 35: K3, P3, K16, P3, K3.

Row 36: Knit.

Row 37: K3, P2, K18, P2, K3.

Row 38: K3, K2tog, K3 (right shoulder), cast off 12 sts, K3 (this includes the st from the last cast off), SSK, K3 (left shoulder). (14 sts)

The right and left shoulders are worked separately

LEFT SHOULDER

Worked over the next 7 sts only.

Row 39: Knit.

Row 40: K2, SSK, K3. (6 sts)

Row 41: Knit.

Row 42: K2, SSK, K2. (5 sts)

Row 43: Knit.

Cast off.

RIGHT SHOULDER

With WS facing rejoin yarn and work over the 7 sts of right shoulder.

Row 39: Knit.

Row 40: K3, K2tog, K2. (6 sts)

Row 41: Knit.

Row 42: K2, K2tog, K2. (5 sts)

Row 43: Knit.

Cast off.

RIGHT FRONT

With WS facing rejoin yarn and work over the remaining 16 sts.

Row 21: K3, P10, K3.

Row 22: K11, K2tog, K3. (15 sts)

Row 23: K3, P9, K3.

Row 24: K3, SSK, K5, K2tog, K3. (13 sts)

Row 25: K3, P7, K3.

Row 26: K3, SSK, knit to end. (12 sts)

Row 27: K3, purl to last 3 sts, K3.

Rows 28–37: Rpt Rows 26–27 5 more times. (7 sts)

Row 38: K3, SSK, K2. (6 sts)

Row 39: Knit.

Row 40: K3, SSK, K1. (5 sts)

Rows 41–43: Knit 3 rows.

Cast off.

MAKING UP

1. Block the waistcoat.

2. Sew shoulder seams.

3. Sew buttons in place on right-hand button band, matching them up with the buttonholes.

4. Sew a button in the centre of each pocket (the garter stitch band just above the central line of decreases on each front).

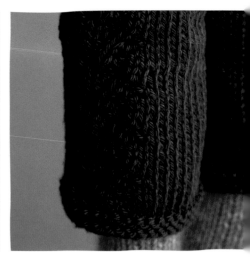

CABLE SHORTS

The shorts are worked top down with no seams. The top part is worked back and forth with a button band down the back and some short row shaping for the bottom; the lower half and legs are worked in the round.

Using 3mm straight needles and Yarn B, cast on 52 sts.

Row 1 (ws): Knit.

Row 2: Knit.

Row 3 (buttonhole row): Knit to last 3 sts, K2tog, YO, K1.

Rows 4–5: Knit 2 rows.

Change to 3.5mm straight needles.

Row 6: [K1, K1fb] 11 times, K1fb 3 times, K1, K1fb 4 times, [K1, K1fb] 10 times, K2. (80 sts)

Row 7: K2, P8, turn.

Row 8: YO, knit to end.

Row 9: K2, P8, SSP, P2, turn.

Row 10: YO, knit to end.

Row 11: K2, P11, SSP, P2, turn.

Row 12: YO, knit to end.

Row 13: K2, P14, SSP, P2, turn.

Row 14: YO, knit to end.

Row 15: K2, P17, SSP, purl to last 2 sts, K2.

Row 16: K10, turn.

Row 17: YO, purl to last 2 sts, K2.

Row 18: K10, K2tog, K2, turn.

Row 19 (buttonhole row): YO, purl to last 3 sts, P2tog, YO, K1.

Row 20: K13, K2tog, K2, turn.

Row 21: YO, purl to last 2 sts, K2.

Row 22: K16, K2tog, K2, turn.

Row 23: YO, purl to last 2 sts, K2.

Row 24: K19, K2tog, knit to end.

Row 25: K2, P15, P1fb, P4, P1fb, P3, P1fb, P2, place pattern marker, P23, P1fb, P3, P1fb, P4, P1fb, P2, place pattern marker, P14, K2. (86 sts)

Row 26: [Knit to pattern marker, C4F, K8, C4B] twice, knit to end.

Row 27 (buttonhole row): K2, purl to last 3 sts, P2tog, YO, K1.

Row 28: [Knit to pattern marker, K2, C4F, K4, C4B, K2] twice, knit to end.

Row 29: K2, purl to last 2 sts, K2.

Row 30: [Knit to pattern marker, K4, C4F, C4B, K4] twice, knit to end.

Row 31: K2, purl to last 2 sts, K2.

Row 32: Transfer sts to a 3.5mm circular needle, [Knit to pattern marker, C4F, K8, C4B] twice, knit to last 2 sts, slip the last 2 sts (without working them) onto a cable needle.

Join to work in the round:

Rnd 33: Position the cable needle behind the first 2 sts on the LH needle, knit first st on LH needle together with first st on cable needle, place marker for beginning of round, knit next st on LH needle together with remaining st on cable needle, knit to end. (84 sts)

Rnd 34: [Knit to pattern marker, K2, C4F, K4, C4B, K2] twice, knit to end.

Rnd 35: Knit.

Rnd 36: [Knit to pattern marker, K4, C4F, C4B, K4] twice, knit to end.

Rnd 37: Knit.

Rnd 38: K1, m1l, [knit to pattern marker, C4F, K8, C4B] twice, knit to last st, m1r, K1. (86 sts)

Rnd 39: Knit.

Rnd 40: [Knit to pattern marker, K2, C4F, K4, C4B, K2] twice, knit to end.

Rnd 41: K1, m1l, knit to last st, m1r, K1. (88 sts)

Rnd 42: Knit to pattern marker, K4, C4F, C4B, K14, m1r, K2, m1l, knit to pattern marker, K4, C4F, C4B, knit to end. (90 sts)

Rnd 43: K1, m1l, knit to last st, m1r, K1. (92 sts)

Rnd 44: [Knit to pattern marker, C4F, K8, C4B] twice, knit to end.

Rnd 45: K1, m1l, K44, m1r, K2, m1l, K44, m1r, K1. (96 sts)

Rnd 46: [Knit to pattern marker, K2, C4F, K4, C4B, K2] twice, knit to end.

Rnd 47: K1, m1l, K46, m1r, K2, m1l, K46, m1r, K1. (100 sts)

Rnd 48: [Knit to pattern marker, K4, C4F, C4B, K4] twice, knit to end.

Divide for legs:

Rnd 49: K50 (right leg), without working them place next 50 sts onto waste yarn (left leg).

RIGHT LEG

Rnd 50: Knit to pattern marker, C4F, K8, C4B, knit to end.

Rnd 51: Knit.

Rnd 52: Knit to pattern marker, K2, C4F, K4, C4B, K2, knit to end.

Rnd 53: Knit.

Rnd 54: SSK, knit to 2 sts before pattern marker, K2tog, K4, C4F, C4B, K4, knit to end. (48 sts)

Rnd 55: Knit.

Rnds 56–67: Rpt Rnds 50–55 twice more. (44 sts)

Rnds 68–71: Rpt Rnds 50–53.

Rnd 72: Knit to pattern marker, K4, C4F, C4B, K4, knit to end.

Change to 3mm circular needle.

Rnd 73: K14, [SSK, K4, K2tog] twice, knit to end. (40 sts)

Rnd 74: Purl.

Rnd 75: Knit.

Rnd 76: Purl.

Cast off.

LEFT LEG

Rnd 49: Transfer sts from waste yarn to 3.5mm circular needle, rejoin yarn and knit 1 rnd placing marker for beginning of rnd.

Rnd 50: Knit to pattern marker, C4F, K8, C4B, knit to end.

Rnd 51: Knit.

Rnd 52: Knit to pattern marker, K2, C4F, K4, C4B, K2, knit to end.

Rnd 53: Knit.

Rnd 54: Knit to pattern marker, K4, C4F, C4B, K4, SSK, knit to last 2 sts, K2tog. (48 sts)

Rnd 55: Knit.

Rnds 56–67: Rpt Rnds 50–55 twice more. (44 sts)

Rnds 68–71: Rpt Rnds 50–53.

Rnds 72–76: Work as Rnds 72–76 of Right Leg.

Cast off.

MAKING UP

1. If necessary, close hole where the 2 legs join with a couple of stitches.

2. Block shorts.

3. Sew buttons in place on left-hand button band down back of pants, matching them up with the buttonholes.

T-BAR SHOES

Using 2.75mm needles and Yarn A for the soles, follow the pattern for the T-Bar Shoes (see Shoes and Accessories), changing to Yarn C for the upper part of the shoes.

HOLLY
THE HEDGEHOG

Hedgehogs have to be so careful when they get dressed in the morning. Holly's frock is new and particularly beautiful – she loves the patterned hem and crossover straps. Life's tricky with prickles!

YOU WILL NEED

FOR HOLLY'S BODY

• Scheepjes Stonewashed (50g/130m; 78% cotton/22% acrylic) yarn in the following shades:

- **Yarn A** Brown (Brown Agate 822), 1 ball

- **Yarn B** Ecru (Axinite 831), 1 ball

• 2.75mm (US 2) straight needles

• Toy stuffing

• 2 x 10mm (½in) buttons

• Scrap piece of 4-ply yarn for embroidering nose

FOR HOLLY'S OUTFIT

• Scheepjes Catona (10g/25m, 25g/62m or 50g/125m; 100% cotton) yarn in the following shades:

- **Yarn A** Light Pink (Old Rose 408), 1 x 50g ball

- **Yarn B** Cream (Old Lace 130), 1 x 25g ball

- **Yarn C** Dark Brown (Black Coffee 162), 1 x 10g ball

- **Yarn D** Mid Brown (Chocolate 507), 1 x 10g ball

• 3mm (US 2½) straight needles

• 3mm (US 2½) circular needle (23cm/9in length)

• Set of four 3mm (US 2½) double-pointed needles

• 3.5mm (US 4) straight needles

• 3.5mm (US 4) circular needle (23cm/9in length)

• Set of four 3.5mm (US 4) double-pointed needles

• Cable needle

• Waste yarn

• 10 small buttons

Before you start, please read the Essential Notes at the beginning of this book.

HEDGEHOG PATTERN

For 'MS' (make spike), cast on 4 sts using the Knit cast-on method (see Techniques: Casting On and Stitches), then knit 5 sts, casting off the first 4 sts as you work them.

HEAD

Starting at neck:

Using Yarn A and 2.75mm straight needles, cast on 11 sts.

Row 1 (ws): (A) P4, (B) P3, (A) P4.

Row 2: (A) [K1, M1] 3 times, K1, (B) [M1, K1] 3 times, M1, (A) [K1, M1] 3 times, K1. (21 sts)

Row 3: (A) P7, (B) P7, (A) P7.

Row 4: (A) [K2, M1] 3 times, K1, (B) K1, M1, [K2, M1] 3 times, (A) [K2, M1] 3 times, K1. (31 sts)

Row 5: (A) P10, (B) P11, (A) P10.

Row 6: (A) K1, m1l, K9, (B) K5, m1r, K1, m1l, K5, (A) K9, m1r, K1. (35 sts)

Row 7: (A) P11, (B) P13, (A) P11.

Row 8: (A) MS, m1l, K1, [MS, K3] twice, (B) K7, m1r, K1, m1l, K7, (A) [K3, MS] twice, K1, m1r, K1. (39 sts)

Row 9: (A) P11, (B) P8, m1pl, P1, m1pr, P8, (A) P11. (41 sts)

Row 10: (A) K1, m1l, [MS, K3] twice, MS, K1, (B) K9, m1r, K1, m1l, K9, (A) K1, MS, [K3, MS] twice, m1r, K1. (45 sts)

Row 11: (A) P12, (B) P10, m1pl, P1, m1pr, P10, (A) P12. (47 sts)

Row 12: (A) K1, m1l, [MS, K2] twice, K1, MS, K2, (B) K12, m1r, K1, m1l, K12, (A) [K2, MS, K1] twice, K1, MS, m1r, K1. (51 sts)

Row 13: (A) P12, (B) P13, m1pl, P1, m1pr, P13, (A) P12. (53 sts)

Row 14: (A) MS, K2, [MS, K3] twice, MS, (B) K14, m1r, K1, m1l, K14, (A) [MS, K3] 3 times. (55 sts)

Row 15: (A) P12, (B) P31, (A) P12.

Row 16: (A) K1, m1l, [MS, K3] twice, MS, K2, (B) K15, m1r, K1, m1l, K15, (A) K2, [MS, K3] twice, MS, m1r, K1. (59 sts)

Row 17: (A) P13, (B) P33, (A) P13.

Row 18: (A) [MS, K3] 3 times, MS, (B) K16, sl1, K16, (A) [MS, K3] 3 times, K1.

Row 19: (A) P13, (B) P33, (A) P13.

Row 20: (A) K2, [MS, K3] twice, MS, K2, (B) K15, CDD, K15, (A) K2, [MS, K3] twice, MS, K2. (57 sts)

Row 21: (A) P13, (B) P31, (A) P13.

Row 22: (A) [MS, K3] 3 times, MS, (B) K14, CDD, K14, (A) [MS, K3] 3 times, K1. (55 sts)

Row 23: (A) P13, (B) P13, PCDD, P13, (A) P13. (53 sts)

Row 24: (A) K2, [MS, K3] twice, MS, K2, (B) K12, CDD, K12, (A) K2, [MS, K3] twice, MS, K2. (51 sts)

Row 25: (A) P13, (B) P11, PCDD, P11, (A) P13. (49 sts)

Row 26: (A) [MS, K3] 3 times, MS, (B) K10, CDD, K10, (A) [MS, K3] 3 times, K1. (47 sts)

Row 27: (A) P14, (B) P8, PCDD, P8, (A) P14. (45 sts)

Row 28: (A) K1, K2tog, MS, K2, [MS, K3] twice, (B) K7, CDD, K7, (A) [K3, MS] twice, K2, MS, SSK, K1. (41 sts)

Row 29: (A) P13, (B) P15, (A) P13.

Row 30: (A) MS, K2, [MS, K3] twice, MS, K1, (B) K7, sl1, K7, (A) K1, [MS, K3] 3 times.

Row 31: (A) P14, (B) P6, (A) P1, (B) P6, (A) P14.

Row 32: (A) MS, K2tog, K2, [MS, K3] twice, MS, (B) K5, (A) K3, (B) K5, (A) [MS, K3] twice, MS, K2, SSK, K1. (39 sts)

Row 33: (A) P14, (B) P3, (A) P5, (B) P3, (A) P14.

Continue in Yarn A only.

Row 34: K2, [MS, K3] 3 times, [MS, K2] twice, K1, MS, K2, [MS, K3] 3 times, MS, K2.

Row 35: Purl.

Row 36: MS, K2tog, K1, [MS, K3] 3 times, [MS, K2] twice, [MS, K3] 3 times, MS, K1, SSK, K1. (37 sts)

Row 37: Purl.

Row 38: K1, [MS, K3] 3 times, [MS, K2] twice, K1, MS, K2, [MS, K3] 3 times, MS, K1.

Row 39: P1, SSP, P3, SSP 4 times, P3, PCDD, P3, P2tog 4 times, P3, P2tog, P1. (25 sts)

Row 40: [K2, MS] twice, K3, [MS, K2] twice, MS, K3, [MS, K2] twice.

Row 41: P1, SSP 5 times, PCDD, P2tog 5 times, P1. (13 sts)

Row 42: K1, *[K1, MS] twice, K2, rpt from *.

Row 43: Purl.

Cast off.

BODY

Using Yarn A and 2.75mm straight needles, cast on 8 sts.

Rows 1-17: As Rows 1-17 of Standard Body – Plain (see Standard Body Parts).

Row 18: (A) K2, [MS, K3] 4 times, MS, K2, (B) K22, (A) K2, [MS, K3] 4 times, MS, K2.

Row 19: (A) P21, (B) P22, (A) P21.

Row 20: (A) [MS, K3] 5 times, MS, (B) K22, (A) [MS, K3] 5 times, K1.

Row 21: (A) P21, (B) P22, (A) P21.

Rows 22-36: Rpt last 4 rows 3 more times, then rpt Rows 18-20 again.

Row 37: (A) P1, SSP, P16, SSP, (B) P2tog, P18, SSP, (A) P2tog, P16, P2tog, P1. (58 sts)

Row 38: (A) [K2, MS] twice, [K3, MS] 3 times, K1, (B) K20, (A) K1, [MS, K3] 3 times, [MS, K2] twice.

Row 39: (A) P19, (B) P20, (A) P19.

Row 40: (A) MS, K2, [MS, K3] 4 times, (B) K20, (A) [K3, MS] 4 times, K3.

Row 41: (A) P19, (B) P20, (A) P19.

Rows 42-46: Rpt last 4 rows once more, then rpt Row 38 again.

Row 47: (A) P1, SSP, P14, SSP, (B) P2tog, P16, SSP, (A) P2tog, P14, P2tog, P1. (52 sts)

Row 48: (A) K2, [MS, K3] 3 times, MS, K2, (B) K18, (A) K2, [MS, K3] 3 times, MS, K2.

Row 49: (A) P17, (B) P18, (A) P17.

Row 50: (A) [MS, K3] 4 times, MS, (B) K18, (A) [MS, K3] 4 times, K1.

Row 51: (A) P17, (B) P18, (A) P17.

Rows 52-54: Rpt Rows 48-50.

Row 55: (A) P1, SSP, P12, SSP, (B) P2tog, P14, SSP, (A) P2tog, P12, P2tog, P1. (46 sts)

Row 56: (A) [K2, MS] twice, [K3, MS] twice, K1, (B) K16, (A) K1, [MS, K3] twice, [MS, K2] twice.

Row 57: (A) P15, (B) P16, (A) P15.

Row 58: (A) [K3, MS] 3 times, K3, (B) K16, (A) [K3, MS] 3 times, K3.

Row 59: (A) P15, (B) P16, (A) P15.

Row 60: As Row 56.

Row 61: (A) P1, SSP, P10, SSP, (B) P2tog, P12, SSP, (A) P2tog, P10, P2tog, P1. (40 sts)

Row 62: (A) K2, [MS, K3] twice, K3, (B) K14, (A) K3, [K3, MS] twice, K2.

Row 63: (A) P13, (B) P14, (A) P13.

Row 64: (A) [MS, K3] twice, K5, (B) K14, (A) K8, MS, K4.

Row 65: (A) P13, (B) P14, (A) P13.

Row 66: As Row 62.

Row 67: (A) P1, SSP, P8, SSP, (B) P2tog, P10, SSP, (A) P2tog, P8, P2tog, P1. (34 sts)

Row 68: (A) [MS, K2] twice, K5, (B) K12, (A) K7, MS, K3.

Row 69: (A) P11, (B) P12, (A) P11.

Row 70: (A) K2, MS, K8, (B) K12, (A) K8, MS, K2.

Row 71: (A) P1, SSP, P6, SSP, (B) P2tog, P8, SSP, (A) P2tog, P6, P2tog, P1. (28 sts)

Row 72: (A) K2, MS, K6, (B) K10, (A) K6, MS, K2.

Row 73: (A) P9, (B) P10, (A) P9.

Row 74: (A) K9, (B) K10, (A) K9.

Row 75: (A) P9, (B) P10, (A) P9.

Row 76: (A) [K1, K2tog] 3 times, (B) [K1, K2tog] 3 times, K1, (A) [K2tog, K1] 3 times. (19 sts)

Row 77: (A) P6, (B) P7, (A) P6.

Row 78: (A) K2tog 3 times, (B) K2tog 3 times, K1, (A) K2tog 3 times. (10 sts)

Row 79: (A) Purl.

Cut yarn leaving a long tail. Using a tapestry needle, thread tail through the stitches left on needle and pull up tight to gather stitches.

ARMS (MAKE 2)

Using Yarn B, work as Standard Arms (see Standard Body Parts).

LEGS (MAKE 2)

Using Yarn B, work as Standard Legs – Plain (see Standard Body Parts).

OUTFIT PATTERNS

LEAF PINAFORE

The pinafore is worked from the bottom up, back and forth with a small seam and button band down the back.

LEAF EDGING

Using Yarn A and 3mm straight needles, cast on 6 sts.

Set-up row (ws): P4, K2.

Row 1: K3, YO, K1, YO, K2. (8 sts)

Row 2: P6, K1fb, K1. (9 sts)

Row 3: K2, P1, K2, YO, K1, YO, K3. (11 sts)

Row 4: P8, K1fb, K2. (12 sts)

Row 5: K2, P2, K3, YO, K1, YO, K4. (14 sts)

Row 6: P10, K1fb, K3. (15 sts)

Row 7: K2, P3, SSK, K5, K2tog, K1. (13 sts)

Row 8: P8, K1fb, P1, K3. (14 sts)

Row 9: K2, P1, K1, P2, SSK, K3, K2tog, K1. (12 sts)

Row 10: P6, K1fb, K1, P1, K3. (13 sts)

Row 11: K2, P1, K1, P3, SSK, K1, K2tog, K1. (11 sts)

Row 12: P4, K1fb, K2, P1, K3. (12 sts)

Row 13: K2, P1, K1, P4, sl1 kw, K2tog, PSSO, K1. (10 sts)

Row 14: Casting off the first 3 sts as you work them: P2tog, K4, P1, K3. (6 sts)

Rows 15-169: Rpt Rows 1-14 11 more times.

Row 170: Knit.

Cast off purlwise.

SKIRT

Using 3mm straight needles and with right side of leaf edging facing you, pick up 86 sts (without working them) along the top edge: starting at the cast-off end of the leaf edging, slide your needle through the first row of purl bumps (photo 1), there are 7 purl bumps for each leaf repeat, plus 1 extra at the start and end of edging.

Set-up row: [K4, K1fb] to last st, K1. (103 sts)

Row 1 (ws): Knit.

Row 2: [K2tog, YO] to last st, K1.

Row 3: Knit.

Change to 3.5mm straight needles.

Rows 4-14: Stocking stitch 11 rows.

Row 15: Cast on 1 st, K2, purl to last st, K1. (104 sts)

Row 16: Cast on 1 st, knit to end. (105 sts)

Row 17: K2, purl to last 2 sts, K2.

Row 18: Knit.

Rows 19-20: Rpt the last 2 rows once more.

Row 21 (buttonhole row): K1, YO, SSP, purl to last 2 sts, K2.

Row 22: Knit.

Row 23: K2, purl to last 2 sts, K2.

Rows 24-28: Rpt last 2 rows twice more, then rpt Row 24 again.

Row 29 (buttonhole row): K1, YO, SSP, purl to last 2 sts, K2.

Row 30: Knit.

Row 31: K2, purl to last 2 sts, K2.

Row 32: K2, [SSK, K1] 15 times, SSK twice, CDD, K2tog twice, [K1, K2tog] 15 times, K2. (69 sts)

Row 33: K25, P19, K25.

Row 34: Knit.

Row 35-36: Rpt last 2 rows once more.

Row 37 (buttonhole row): K1, YO, K2tog, K22, P19, knit to end.

Row 38: Cast off 22 sts, K3, SSK, K15, K2tog, K3, cast off 22 sts. (23 sts)

FRONT BIB

Rejoin yarn to remaining 23 sts.

Row 39: K3, purl to last 3 sts, K3.

Row 40: Knit.

Rows 41-43: Rpt last 2 rows, then rpt Row 41.

Row 44: K3, SSK, knit to last 5 sts, K2tog, K3. (21 sts)

Rows 45-56: Rpt Rows 39-44 twice more. (17 sts)

Row 57: Knit.

Row 58 (buttonhole row): K2, YO, K2tog, K9, SSK, YO, K2.

Row 59: Knit.

Cast off.

POCKET

Using Yarn A and 3mm straight needles, cast on 9 sts.

Row 1 (ws): Knit.

Change to 3.5mm straight needles.

Rows 2–9: Stocking stitch 8 rows.

Cast off.

STRAPS (MAKE 2)

Using 3.5mm straight needles, with RS facing, and leaving a gap of 6 sts between the edge of the strap and the edge of the button band opening, pick up and knit 4 sts along the waist cast-off edge. To do this, insert right-hand needle under the horizontal 'V' of the cast-off stitch, wrap yarn around needle and pull through as if to knit. Repeat for next 3 sts.

Row 1 (ws): Knit.

Rows 2-45: Knit 44 rows.

Row 46: K2tog, SSK. (2 sts)

Cut yarn leaving a short tail. Using a tapestry needle, thread tail through the stitches left on needle and pull up tight to gather stitches. Weave in tail on back of strap. Repeat for second strap.

MAKING UP

1. Block pinafore and pocket.

2. Sew centre back edges together, starting at the bottom of the leaf edging and ending at the bottom of the button band.

3. Sew buttons in place on left-hand button band and at the end of each strap (on right side), matching them up with the buttonholes.

4. Position the pocket on the front centre of the pinafore bib and pin in place. Sew around three sides, leaving the top of the pocket open.

FRENCH KNICKERS

Using Yarn B, follow the pattern for the French Knickers (see Shoes and Accessories).

MARY JANE SHOES

Using Yarn C for the soles and changing to Yarn D for the upper parts of the shoes, follow the pattern for the Mary Jane Shoes (see Shoes and Accessories).

MAISIE
THE PIG

Maisie picked out this textured pink dress because it goes so well with her snout, then threw on her favourite grey cardigan. The starlet shoes were an after-thought. Some people just can't help being stylish.

YOU WILL NEED

FOR MAISIE'S BODY
- Scheepjes Stonewashed (50g/130m; 78% cotton/22% acrylic) yarn in the following shades:

  - *Yarn A Pale Pink (Pink Quartzite 821), 2 balls*

  - *Yarn B Pink (Rose Quartz 820), 1 ball*

- 2.75mm (US 2) straight needles

- Toy stuffing

- 2 x 10mm (½in) buttons

- Scrap piece of 4-ply yarn for embroidering nostrils

FOR MAISIE'S OUTFIT
- Scheepjes Catona (10g/25m, 25g/62m or 50g/125m; 100% cotton) yarn in the following shades:

  - *Yarn A Light Pink (Old Rose 408), 1 x 50g and 1 x 10g ball*

  - *Yarn B Dark Grey (Metal Grey 242), 1 x 50g ball*

  - *Yarn C Pale Grey (Light Silver 172), 1 x 25g ball*

- 3mm (US 2½) straight needles

- 3mm (US 2½) circular needle (23cm/9in length)

- Set of four 3mm (US 2½) double-pointed needles

- 3.5mm (US 4) straight needles

- 3.5mm (US 4) circular needle (23cm/9in length)

- Set of four 3.5mm (US 4) double-pointed needles

- Cable needle

- Waste yarn

- 12 small buttons

Before you start, please read the Essential Notes at the beginning of this book.

PIG PATTERN

HEAD

Starting at neck:

Using Yarn A and 2.75mm straight needles, cast on 11 sts.

Row 1 (ws): Purl.

Row 2: [K1, M1] to last st, K1. (21 sts)

Row 3: Purl.

Row 4: [K2, M1] to last st, K1. (31 sts)

Row 5: Purl.

Row 6: K1, m1l, knit to last st, m1r, K1. (33 sts)

Row 7: P16, P1 and place a removable marker around this stitch on RS, P16.

Row 8: [K1, m1l, K15, m1r] twice, K1. (37 sts)

Row 9: Purl.

Row 10: [K1, m1l, K17, m1r] twice, K1. (41 sts)

Row 11: Purl.

Row 12: [K1, m1l, K19, m1r] twice, K1. (45 sts)

Row 13: Purl.

Row 14: K22, m1r, K1, m1l, K22. (47 sts)

Row 15: Purl.

Row 16: K1, m1l, knit to last st, m1r, K1. (49 sts)

Rows 17–19: Stocking stitch 3 rows.

Row 20: K17, *K1 and place a removable marker around this stitch*, K13, rpt from * to *, K17.

Rows 21–25: Stocking stitch 5 rows.

Row 26: K23, CDD, K23. (47 sts)

Row 27: Purl.

Row 28: K1, K2tog, K19, CDD, K19, SSK, K1. (43 sts)

Row 29: Purl.

Row 30: K20, CDD, K20. (41 sts)

Row 31: P20, P1 and place a removable marker around this stitch on RS, P20.

Row 32: K1, K2tog, K17, sl1, K17, SSK, K1. (39 sts)

Row 33: Purl.

Row 34: K19, sl1, K19.

Row 35: Purl.

Row 36: K1, K2tog, K16, sl1, K16, SSK, K1. (37 sts)

Row 37: Purl.

Row 38: K18, sl1, K18.

Row 39: Purl.

Row 40: K1, K2tog, K3, K2tog 4 times, K3, CDD, K3, SSK 4 times, K3, SSK, K1. (25 sts)

Row 41: Purl.

Row 42: K1, K2tog 5 times, CDD, SSK 5 times, K1. (13 sts)

Row 43: Purl.

Cast off.

SNOUT

Using Yarn A and 2.75mm straight needles, cast on 31 sts.

Row 1 (ws): Purl.

Rows 2-9: Stocking stitch 8 rows.

Row 10: Purl.

Change to Yarn B.

Row 11: Purl.

Row 12: K4, K2tog 4 times, K7, K2tog 4 times, K4. (23 sts)

Row 13: Purl.

Row 14: K4, K2tog twice, K7, K2tog twice, K4. (19 sts)

Row 15: Purl.

Row 16: K2tog 4 times, CDD, K2tog 4 times. (9 sts)

Cut yarn leaving a long tail. Using a tapestry needle, thread tail through the stitches left on needle and pull up tight to gather stitches.

EARS (MAKE 2)

Using Yarn A and 2.75mm straight needles, cast on 33 sts.

Row 1 (ws): (A) P10, (B) P13, (A) P10.

Row 2: (A) K10, (B) K13, (A) K10.

Rows 3–11: Rpt last 2 rows 4 more times, then rpt Row 1 again.

Row 12: (A) K7, K2tog, K1, (B) SSK, K9, K2tog, (A) K1, SSK, K7. (29 sts)

Row 13: (A) P9, (B) P11, (A) P9.

Row 14: (A) K6, K2tog, K1, (B) SSK, K7, K2tog, (A) K1, SSK, K6. (25 sts)

Row 15: (A) P8, (B) P9, (A) P8.

Row 16: (A) K5, K2tog, K1, (B) SSK, K5, K2tog, (A) K1, SSK, K5. (21 sts)

Row 17: (A) P7, (B) P7, (A) P7.

Row 18: (A) K4, K2tog, K1, (B) SSK, K3, K2tog, (A) K1, SSK, K4. (17 sts)

Row 19: (A) P6, (B) P5, (A) P6.

Row 20: (A) K3, K2tog, K1, (B) SSK, K1, K2tog, (A) K1, SSK, K3. (13 sts)

Row 21: (A) P5, (B) P3, (A) P5.

Row 22: (A) K2, K2tog, SSK, (B) K1, (A) K2tog, SSK, K2. (9 sts)

Continue in Yarn A only.

Row 23: Purl.

Row 24: K1, K2tog, K3, SSK, K1. (7 sts)

Cut yarn leaving a long tail. Using a tapestry needle, thread tail through the stitches left on needle and pull up tight to gather stitches.

TAIL

Using Yarn A and 2.75mm straight needles, cast on 16 sts.

Row 1 (ws): Purl.

Rows 2–5: Stocking stitch 4 rows.

Row 6: [K1, K2tog, K2, SSK, K1] twice. (12 sts)

Rows 7–9: Stocking stitch 3 rows.

Row 10: [K1, K2tog, SSK, K1] twice. (8 sts)

Rows 11–13: Stocking stitch 3 rows.

Row 14: K7, turn.

Row 15: YO, P6, turn.

Row 16: YO, K5, turn.

Row 17: YO, P4, turn.

Row 18: YO, K3, turn.

Row 19: YO, P2, turn.

Row 20: YO, K2, K2tog 3 times.

Row 21: P5, SSP 3 times.

Rows 22–69: Rpt Rows 14-21 6 more times.

Rows 70–79: Stocking stitch 10 rows.

Row 80: K1, K2tog 3 times, K1. (5 sts)

Row 81: Purl.

Cut yarn leaving a long tail. Using a tapestry needle, thread tail through the stitches left on needle and pull up tight to gather stitches.

BODY

Work as Standard Body – Plain (see Standard Body Parts).

ARMS (MAKE 2)

Work as Standard Arms (see Standard Body Parts).

LEGS (MAKE 2)

Work as Standard Leg – Plain (see Standard Body Parts).

MAKING UP

Follow the instructions in the techniques section (see Techniques: Making Up Your Animal).

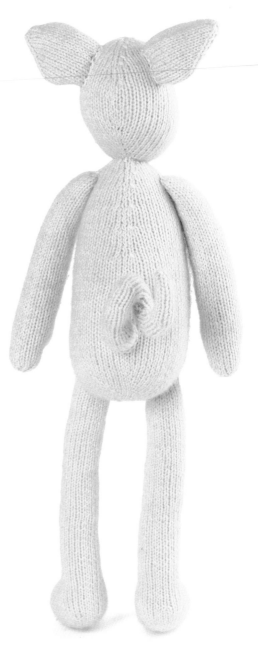

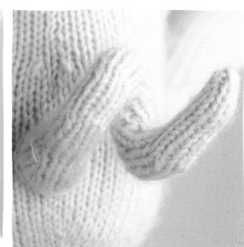

OUTFIT PATTERNS

DRESS

The dress is worked top down, seamlessly with a round yoke. The top half is worked back and forth with a button band down the back and the bottom half is worked in the round.

Using Yarn A and 3mm straight needles, cast on 31 sts.

Row 1 (ws): Knit.

Row 2 (buttonhole row): K1, YO, K2tog, knit to end.

Row 3: Knit.

Change to 3.5mm straight needles.

Row 4: K3, K1fb to last 4 sts, K4. (55 sts)

Row 5: K3, purl to last 3 sts, K3.

Rows 6–7: Knit 2 rows.

Row 8: K3, [K1, K1fb, K1] to last 4 sts, K4. (71 sts)

Rows 9–11: Rpt Rows 5–7.

Row 12: K3, [K1, K1fb, K2] to last 4 sts, K4. (87 sts)

Rows 13–15: Rpt Rows 5–7.

Row 16 (buttonhole row): K1, YO, K2tog, [K2, K1fb, K2] to last 4 sts, K4. (103 sts)

Rows 17–19: Rpt Rows 5–7.

Row 20: K3, [K2, K1fb, K3] to last 4 sts, K4. (119 sts)

Rows 21–23: Rpt Rows 5–7.

Row 24: K18, cast off 25 sts, K13, K1fb 6 times, K14, cast off 25 sts, K18. (75 sts)

Row 25: K3, P16, pm, P39, pm, purl to last 3 sts, K3.

Row 26: [Knit to marker, m1r, sm, K2, m1l] twice, knit to end. (79 sts)

Row 27: K3, purl to last 3 sts, K3.

Row 28: Knit.

Row 29: As Row 27.

Row 30 (buttonhole row): K1, YO, K2tog, [knit to marker, m1r, sm, K2, m1l] twice, knit to end. (83 sts)

Rows 31–33: Rpt Rows 27–29.

Rows 34–41: Rpt Rows 26–29 twice. (91 sts)

Row 42 (buttonhole row): As Row 30. (95 sts)

Rows 43–45: Rpt Rows 27–29.

Row 46–49: Rpt Rows 26–29. (99 sts)

Rows 50–51: Rpt Rows 27–28.

Rows 52–53: Rpt Rows 26–27. (103 sts)

Row 54: Transfer sts to a 3.5mm circular needle, knit to last 3 sts, slip the last 3 sts (without working them) onto a cable needle.

Join to work in the round:

Rnd 55: Position cable needle behind first 3 sts on LH needle, knit first st on LH needle together with first st on cable needle, rpt for second st, place marker for beginning of round, knit next st on LH needle together with remaining st on cable needle, knit to end. (100 sts)

Rnd 56–57: Knit 2 rnds.

Rnd 58: [YO, K8, K2tog] to end.

Rnd 59: Knit.

Rnd 60: [K1, YO, SSK, K5, K2tog, YO] to end.

Rnd 61: Knit.

Rnd 62: [K2, YO, SSK, K3, K2tog, YO, K1] to end.

Rnd 63: Knit.

Rnd 64: *K1, [YO, SSK] twice, K1, [K2tog, YO] twice; rpt from * to end.

Rnd 65: Knit.

Rnd 66: [K2, YO, SSK, YO, CDD, YO, K2tog, YO, K1] to end.

Rnds 67–78: Rpt last 4 rnds 3 more times.

Rnd 79: Knit.

Cast-off rnd: Cast off 3 sts, *K2tog and cast off this st by passing second st on RH needle over first st (photo 1), slip st from RH needle back onto LH needle, cast on 2 sts (using knit cast-on method) (photo 2), cast off 10 sts: rpt from * to last 6 sts, K2tog and cast off this st as before, cast off remaining sts.

MAKING UP

1. Block dress.

2. Sew buttons in place on left-hand button band down back of dress, matching them up with the buttonholes.

CARDIGAN

The cardigan is worked top down, seamlessly and with raglan sleeves. The body is worked back and forth in rows and the sleeves are worked in the round.

Using Yarn B and 3mm straight needles, cast on 39 sts.

Row 1 (ws): Knit.

Row 2 (buttonhole row): K1, YO, K2tog, knit to end.

Change to 3.5mm straight needles.

Row 3: K3, P5, pm, P6, pm, P12, pm, P6, pm, P4, K3.

Row 4: K4, YO, SSK, K1, m1r, sm, K1, m1l, K2tog, YO, K1, YO, SSK, m1r, sm, K1, m1l, K1, [K2tog, YO] twice, K1, [YO, SSK] twice, K1, m1r, sm, K1, m1l, K2tog, YO, K1, YO, SSK, m1r, sm, K1, m1l, K1, K2tog, YO, K4. (47 sts)

Row 5: K3, purl to last 3 sts, K3.

Row 6: K5, YO, SSK, K1, m1r, sm, K1, m1l, K2tog, YO, K3, YO, SSK, m1r, sm, K1, m1l, K1, [K2tog, YO] twice, K3, [YO, SSK] twice, K1, m1r, sm, K1, m1l, K2tog, YO, K3, YO, SSK, m1r, sm, K1, m1l, K1, K2tog, YO, K5. (55 sts)

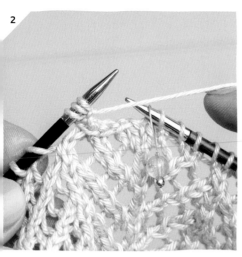

Row 7: As Row 5.

Row 8: K4, [YO, SSK] twice, K1, m1r, sm, K1, m1l, [K2tog, YO] twice, K1, [YO, SSK] twice, m1r, sm, K1, m1l, K3, [K2tog, YO] twice, K1, [YO, SSK] twice, K3, m1r, sm, K1, m1l, [K2tog, YO] twice, K1, [YO, SSK] twice, m1r, sm, K1, m1l, K1, [K2tog, YO] twice, K4. (63 sts)

Row 9: As Row 5.

Row 10 (buttonhole row): K1, YO, K2tog, K2, [YO, SSK] twice, K1, m1r, sm, K1, m1l, [K2tog, YO] twice, K3, [YO, SSK] twice, m1r, sm, K1, m1l, K3, [K2tog, YO] twice, K1, [YO, SSK] twice, K3, m1r, sm, K1, m1l, [K2tog, YO] twice, K3, [YO, SSK] twice, m1r, sm, K1, m1l, K1, [K2tog, YO] twice, K5. (71 sts)

Row 11: K3, P21, [place pattern marker, P17] twice, place pattern marker, purl to last 3 sts, K3.

Row 12: K4, [YO, SSK] twice, *knit to marker, m1r, sm, K1, m1l, knit to pattern marker, sm, K1, [K2tog, YO] twice, K1, [YO, SSK] twice; rep from * twice more, knit to marker, m1r, sm, K1, m1l, knit to last 8 sts, [K2tog, YO] twice, K4. (79 sts)

Row 13: As Row 5.

Row 14: K5, [YO, SSK] twice, *knit to marker, m1r, sm, K1, m1l, knit to pattern marker, sm, [K2tog, YO] twice, K3, [YO, SSK] twice; rep from * twice more, knit to marker, m1r, sm, K1, m1l, knit to last 9 sts, [K2tog, YO] twice, K5. (87 sts)

Row 15: As Row 5.

Rows 16–17: Rpt Rows 12–13. (95 sts)

Row 18 (buttonhole row): K1, YO, K2tog, K2, [YO, SSK] twice, *knit to marker, m1r, sm, K1, m1l, knit to pattern marker, sm, [K2tog, YO] twice, K3, [YO, SSK] twice; rep from * twice more, knit to marker, m1r, sm, K1, m1l, knit to last 9 sts, [K2tog, YO] twice, K5. (103 sts)

Row 19: As Row 5.

Rows 20–23: Rpt Rows 12–15. (119 sts)

Row 24: K4, [YO, SSK] twice, knit to marker, sm, K1 (left front), without working them place next 25 sts and pattern marker onto waste yarn (sleeve), remove marker, knit to pattern marker, sm, K1, [K2tog, YO] twice, K1, [YO, SSK] twice, knit to marker, sm, K1 (back), without working them place next 25 sts and pattern marker onto waste yarn (sleeve), remove marker, knit to last 8 sts, [K2tog, YO] twice, K4 (right front). (69 sts)

Row 25: As Row 5.

Row 26: K5, [YO, SSK] twice, knit to marker, m1r, sm, K2, m1l, knit to pattern marker, sm, [K2tog, YO] twice, K3, [YO, SSK] twice, knit to marker, m1r, sm, K2, m1l, knit to last 9 sts, [K2tog, YO] twice, K5. (73 sts)

Row 27: As Row 5.

Row 28: K4, [YO, SSK] twice, knit to pattern marker, sm, K1, [K2tog, YO] twice, K1, [YO, SSK] twice, knit to last 8 sts, [K2tog, YO] twice, K4.

Rows 29–40: Rpt Rows 25–28 3 more times. (85 sts)

Change to 3mm straight needles.

Rows 41–43: Knit 3 rows.

Cast off.

SLEEVES

Starting at under arm, slip the 25 sts held on waste yarn for one sleeve evenly onto three 3.5mm dpns and rejoin yarn.

Using fourth dpn, start knitting in the round.

Rnd 1: Knit to pattern marker, K1, [K2tog, YO] twice, K1, [YO, SSK] twice, knit to end.

Rnd 2: Knit.

Rnd 3: Knit to pattern marker, [K2tog, YO] twice, K3, [YO, SSK] twice, knit to end.

Rnd 4: K1, m1l, knit to last st, m1r, K1. (27 sts)

Rnds 5–7: Rpt Rnds 1–3.

Rnd 8: Knit.

Rnds 9–12: Rpt Rnds 1–4. (29 sts)

Rnds 13–20: Rpt Rnds 5–8 twice.

Rnd 21: Rpt Rnd 1.

Change to a set of 3mm dpns.

Rnd 22: Purl.

Rnd 23: Knit.

Rnd 24: Purl.

Cast off.

Repeat for second sleeve.

MAKING UP

1. Block cardigan.

2. Sew buttons in place on front right-hand button band, matching them up with the buttonholes.

STARLET SHOES

Using Yarn B for the soles and changing to Yarn A for the upper parts of the shoes, follow the pattern for the Starlet Shoes (see Shoes and Accessories).

FRENCH KNICKERS

Using Yarn C, follow the pattern for the French Knickers (see Shoes and Accessories).

STANLEY
THE RACCOON

Irrepressible Stanley keeps his school teachers on their toes, but now it's the holidays and he's off in search of some seaside fun in his striped shorts, and matching red sneakers and sweater.

YOU WILL NEED

FOR STANLEY'S BODY

- Scheepjes Stonewashed (50g/130m; 78% cotton/22% acrylic) yarn in the following shades:

  - **Yarn A** Grey (Smokey Quartz 802), 2 balls

  - **Yarn B** Cream (Moonstone 801), 1 ball

  - **Yarn C** Black (Black Onyx 803), 1 ball

- 2.75mm (US 2) straight needles
- Toy stuffing
- 2 x 10mm (½in) buttons
- Scrap piece of 4-ply yarn for embroidering nose

FOR STANLEY'S OUTFIT

- Scheepjes Catona (10g/25m, 25g/62m or 50g/125m; 100% cotton) yarn in the following shades:

  - **Yarn A** Red (Candy Apple 516), 1 x 50g ball

  - **Yarn B** Dark Blue (Light Navy 164), 1 x 25g ball

  - **Yarn C** Cream (Old Lace 130), 1 x 25g ball

- 2.75mm (US 2) straight needles
- 3mm (US 2½) straight needles
- 3mm (US 2½) circular needle (23cm/9in length)

- Set of four 3mm (US 2½) double-pointed needles
- 3.5mm (US 4) straight needles
- 3.5mm (US 4) circular needle (23cm/9in length)
- Set of four 3.5mm (US 4) double-pointed needles
- Cable needle
- Waste yarn
- 6 small buttons

Before you start, please read the Essential Notes at the beginning of this book.

RACCOON PATTERN

HEAD

Starting at neck:

Using Yarn A and 2.75mm straight needles, cast on 11 sts.

Row 1 (ws): (A) P4, (B) P3, (A) P4.

Row 2: (A) [K1, M1] 4 times, (B) [K1, M1] 3 times, (A) [K1, M1] 3 times, K1. (21 sts)

Row 3: (A) P7, (B) P6, (A) P8.

Row 4: (A) [K2, M1] 3 times, K2, (B) [M1, K2] 3 times, (A) [M1, K2] 3 times, M1, K1. (31 sts)

Row 5: (A) P11, (B) P9, (A) P11.

Row 6: (A) K1, m1l, K10, (B) K9, (A) K10, m1r, K1. (33 sts)

Row 7: (A) P12, (B) P9, (A) P12.

Row 8: (A) K1, m1l, K10, (B) K5, m1r, K1, m1l, K5, (A) K10, m1r, K1. (37 sts)

Row 9: (A) P12, (B) P13, (A) P12.

Row 10: (A) K1, m1l, K10, (B) K7, m1r, K1, m1l, K7, (A) K10, m1r, K1. (41 sts)

Row 11: (A) P12, (B) P8, m1pl, P1, m1pr, P8, (A) P12. (43 sts)

Row 12: (A) K1, m1l, K10, (B) K10, m1r, K1, m1l, K10, (A) K10, m1r, K1. (47 sts)

Row 13: (A) P12, (B) P11, m1pl, P1, m1pr, P11, (A) P12. (49 sts)

Row 14: (A) K11, (B) K13, m1r, K1, m1l, K13, (A) K11. (51 sts)

Row 15: (A) P11, (B) P14, m1pl, P1, m1pr, P14, (A) P11. (53 sts)

Row 16: (A) K1, m1l, K9, (B) K16, m1r, K1, m1l, K16, (A) K9, m1r, K1. (57 sts)

Row 17: (A) P11, (B) P35, (A) P11.

Row 18: (A) K10, (B) K4, (C) K6, (B) K8, m1r, K1, m1l, K8, (C) K6, (B) K4, (A) K10. (59 sts)

Row 19: (A) P10, (B) P3, (C) P7, (B) P19, (C) P7, (B) P3, (A) P10.

Row 20: (A) K9, (B) K3, (C) K8, (B) K9, sl1, K9, (C) K8, (B) K3, (A) K9.

Row 21: (A) P9, (B) P2, (C) P9, (B) P19, (C) P9, (B) P2, (A) P9.

Row 22: (A) K8, (B) K2, (C) K11, (B) K7, CDD, K7, (C) K11, (B) K2, (A) K8. (57 sts)

Row 23: (A) P8, (B) P2, (C) P11, (B) P15, (C) P11, (B) P2, (A) P8.

Row 24: (A) K9, (B) K2, (C) K10, (B) K6, CDD, K6, (C) K10, (B) K2, (A) K9. (55 sts)

Row 25: (A) P9, (B) P2, (C) P11, (B) P4, PCDD, P4, (C) P11, (B) P2, (A) P9. (53 sts)

Row 26: (A) K10, (B) K2, (C) K10, (B) K3, CDD, K3, (C) K10, (B) K2, (A) K10. (51 sts)

Row 27: (A) P10, (B) P2, (C) P11, (B) P1, PCDD, P1, (C) P11, (B) P2, (A) P10. (49 sts)

Row 28: (A) K1, K2tog, K8, (B) K2, (C) K10, CDD, K10, (B) K2, (A) K8, SSK, K1. (45 sts)

Row 29: (A) P10, (B) P2, (C) P9, PCDD, P9, (B) P2, (A) P10. (43 sts)

Row 30: (A) K11, (B) K2, (C) K7, CDD, K7, (B) K2, (A) K11. (41 sts)

Row 31: (A) P11, (B) P2, (C) P6, (A) P3, (C) P6, (B) P2, (A) P11.

Row 32: (A) K1, K2tog, K9, (B) K2, (C) K5, (A) K1, sl1, K1, (C) K5, (B) K2, (A) K9, SSK, K1. (39 sts)

Row 33: (A) P11, (B) P3, (C) P3, (B) P1, (A) P3, (B) P1, (C) P3, (B) P3, (A) P11.

Row 34: (A) K12, (B) K6, (A) K1, sl1, K1, (B) K6, (A) K12.

Row 35: (A) P12, (B) P6, (A) P3, (B) P6, (A) P12.

Row 36: (A) K1, K2tog, K10, (B) K5, (A) K1, sl1, K1, (B) K5, (A) K10, SSK, K1. (37 sts)

Row 37: (A) P13, (B) P3, (A) P5, (B) P3, (A) P13.

Continue in Yarn A only.

Row 38: K18, sl1, K18.

Row 39: Purl.

Row 40: K1, K2tog, K3, K2tog 4 times, K3, CDD, K3, SSK 4 times, K3, SSK, K1. (25 sts)

Row 41: Purl.

Row 42: K1, K2tog 5 times, CDD, SSK 5 times, K1. (13 sts)

Row 43: Purl.

Cast off.

EARS (MAKE 2)

Using 2.75mm straight needles and Yarn A, cast on 18 sts.

Row 1 (ws): (A) P7, (C) P4, (A) P7.

Row 2: (A) K7, (C) [K1, M1] 3 times, K1, (A) K7. (21 sts)

Row 3: (A) P7, (C) P7, (A) P7.

Row 4: (A) K7, (C) K7, (A) K7.

Row 5: (A) P7, (C) P7, (A) P7.

Row 6: (A) K4, K2tog, K1, (C) SSK, K3, K2tog, (A) K1, SSK, K4. (17 sts)

Row 7: (A) P6, (C) P5, (A) P6.

Row 8: (A) K6, (C) K5, (A) K6.

Row 9: (A) P6, (C) P5, (A) P6.

Row 10: (A) K3, K2tog, K1, (C) SSK, K1, K2tog, (A) K1, SSK, K3. (13 sts)

Row 11: (A) P5, (C) P3, (A) P5.

Continue in Yarn A only.

Row 12: K2, K2tog, SSK, K1, K2tog, SSK, K2. (9 sts)

Row 13: Purl.

Row 14: K1, K2tog, sl1 kw, K2tog, PSSO, SSK, K1. (5 sts)

Cut yarn leaving a long tail. Using a tapestry needle, thread tail through the stitches left on needle and pull up tight to gather stitches.

TAIL

Using 2.75mm straight needles and Yarn A, cast on 19 sts.

Row 1 (ws): Purl.

Rows 2–3: Stocking stitch 2 rows.

Work rows 4-35 in a stripe rpt of 4 rows Yarn C and 4 rows Yarn A, starting with Yarn C.

Rows 4–5: Stocking stitch 2 rows.

Row 6: K4, [M1, K6] twice, M1, K3. (22 sts)

Rows 7–9: Stocking stitch 3 rows.

Row 10: K1, [M1, K7] 3 times. (25 sts)

Rows 11–13: Stocking stitch 3 rows.

Row 14: K3, [M1, K4] 5 times, M1, K2. (31 sts)

Rows 15–33: Stocking stitch 19 rows.

Row 34: K6, SSK, K1, K2tog, K20. (29 sts)

Row 35: Purl.

Continue in Yarn C only.

Row 36: K19, SSK, K1, K2tog, K5. (27 sts)

Row 37: Purl.

Row 38: K5, SSK, K1, K2tog, K17. (25 sts)

Row 39: Purl.

Row 40: [K4, SSK, K1, K2tog, K3] twice, K1. (21 sts)

Row 41: Purl.

Row 42: [K3, SSK, K1, K2tog, K2] twice, K1. (17 sts)

Row 43: Purl.

Row 44: [K2, SSK, K1, K2tog, K1] twice, K1. (13 sts)

Row 45: Purl.

Row 46: [K1, SSK, K1, K2tog] twice, K1. (9 sts)

Row 47: Purl.

Row 48: SSK, K1, K2tog, CDD, K1. (5 sts)

Row 49: Purl.

Cut yarn leaving a long tail. Using a tapestry needle, thread tail through the stitches left on needle and pull up tight to gather stitches.

BODY

Work as Standard Body - Chest Blaze (see Standard Body Parts).

ARMS (MAKE 2)

Work as Standard Arms (see Standard Body Parts).

LEGS (MAKE 2)

Work as Standard Leg - Contrast Foot Pad, but using Yarn C instead of Yarn B for Rows 1-8 (see Standard Body Parts).

MAKING UP

Follow the instructions in the techniques section (see Techniques: Making Up Your Animal).

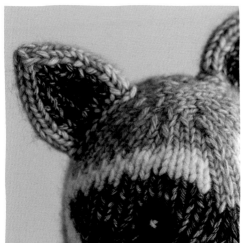

OUTFIT PATTERNS

DIAMOND SWEATER

The sweater is worked top down, with raglan sleeves and no seams. The top half is worked back and forth in rows with a button band opening, the body and sleeves are worked in the round.

Note the following special abbreviations:
'C2B' – Place 1 st on CN, hold to back, slip 1 st purlwise wyib, knit st from CN.
'C2F' – Place 1 st on CN, hold to front, K1, slip 1 st purlwise wyib from CN.

Using Yarn A and 3.5mm straight needles, cast on 36 sts.

Row 1 (ws): Purl.

Rows 2–4: Stocking stitch 3 rows.

Row 5: Cast on 3 sts using Purl cast-on method (see Techniques: Casting On and Stitches), P5, P1fb, P3, pm, P6, P1fb, P5, pm, P2, P1fb, P3, pm, P3, P1fb, purl to end. (43 sts)

Row 6: P3, K1, m1l, K1, C2B, C2F, [knit to marker, m1r, sm, K1, m1l] twice, K4, C2B, C2F, knit to marker, m1r, sm, K1, m1l, knit to last 4 sts, m1r, K1, P3. (51 sts)

Row 7 (buttonhole row): Purl to last 2 sts, YO, P2tog

Row 8: P3, K1, m1l, K1, *C2B, K2, C2F, knit to marker, m1r, sm, K1, m1l, C2F*, K4, C2B, m1r, sm, K1, m1l, K4; rpt from * to * once, K5, m1r, K1, P3. (59 sts)

Row 9: Purl.

Row 10: P3, K1, m1l, K1, *C2B, K4, C2F, K2, C2B, m1r, sm, K1, m1l, K2, C2F, K2, C2B*, K2, m1r, sm, K1, m1l, C2F, K2; rpt from * to * once, K1, m1r, K1, P3. (67 sts)

Row 11: Purl.

Row 12: P3, K1, m1l, K1, *C2B, K6, C2F, C2B, K2, m1r, sm, K1, m1l, K4, C2F, C2B*, K4, m1r, sm, K1, m1l, K2, C2F; rpt from * to * once, K3, m1r, K1, P3. (75 sts)

Row 13 (buttonhole row): As Row 7.

Row 14: P3, K1, m1l, K1, *C2B, K8, C2B, K4, m1r, sm, K1, m1l, K6, C2B*, K6, m1r, sm, K1, m1l, K4; rpt from * to * once, K5, m1r, K1, P3. (83 sts)

Row 15: Purl.

Row 16: P3, K1, m1l, K1, *C2B, C2F, K6, C2B, C2F, K4, m1r, sm, K1, m1l, K6, C2B, C2F*, K6, m1r, sm, K1, m1l, K4; rpt from * to * once, K5, m1r, K1, P3. (91 sts)

Row 17: Purl.

Row 18: P3, K1, m1l, K1, *[C2B, K2, C2F, K4] twice, m1r, sm, K1, m1l, C2F, K4, C2B, K2, C2F*, K4, C2B, m1r, sm, K1, m1l, K4; rpt from * to * once, K5, m1r, K1, P3. (99 sts)

Row 19 (buttonhole row): As Row 7.

Row 20: P3, K1, m1l, K1, *[C2B, K4, C2F, K2] twice, C2B, m1r, sm, K1, m1l, K2, C2F, K2, C2B, K4, C2F, K2, C2B*, K2, m1r, sm, K1, m1l, C2F, K2; rpt from * to * once, K1, m1r, K1, P3. (107 sts)

Row 21: Purl.

Row 22: P3, K1, m1l, K1, *[C2B, K6, C2F] twice, C2B, K2, m1r, sm, K1, m1l, K4, C2F, C2B, K6, C2F, C2B*, K4, m1r, sm, K1, m1l, K2, C2F; rpt from * to * once, K3, m1r, K1, P3. (115 sts)

Row 23: Purl.

Row 24: Transfer sts to a 3.5mm circular needle, P3, K1, m1l, K1, *[C2B, K8] twice, C2B, K4, m1r, sm, K1, m1l, K6, C2B, K8, C2B*, K6, m1r, sm, K1, m1l, K4; rpt from * to * once, K5, m1r, K1, slip the last 3 sts (without working them) onto a cable needle. (123 sts)

Join to work in the round:

Rnd 25: Position cable needle behind first 3 sts on LH needle, place marker for beginning of round, knit first st on LH needle together with first st on cable needle; rpt for next 2 sts, *knit to marker, sm, K1 (back), without working them place next 26 sts onto waste yarn (sleeve)*, remove marker; rpt from * to * once (front and sleeve). (68 sts)

Rnd 26: K1, m1l, *K4, C2B, [C2F, K6, C2B] twice, C2F*, knit to marker, sm, K2, m1l; rpt from * to * once, knit to last st, m1r, K1. (72 sts)

Rnd 27: Knit.

Rnd 28: *K5, [C2B, K2, C2F, K4] 3 times, K1; rpt from * once more.

Rnd 29: Knit.

Rnd 30: K1, m1l, *K3, [C2B, K4, C2F, K2] twice, C2B, K4, C2F*, knit to marker, m1r, sm, K2, m1l; rpt from * to * once, knit to last st, m1r, K1. (76 sts)

Rnd 31: Knit.

Rnd 32: *K2, [C2F, C2B, K6] 3 times, C2F, C2B, K2; rpt from * once more.

Rnd 33: Knit.

Rnd 34: K1, m1l, *K2, [C2B, K8] 3 times, C2B*, knit to marker, m1r, sm, K2, m1l; rpt from * to * once, knit to last st, m1r, K1. (80 sts)

Rnd 35: Knit.

Rnd 36: K3, [C2B, C2F, K6] 7 times, C2B, C2F, K3.

Rnd 37: Knit.

Rnd 38: K1, m1l, *K1, [C2B, K2, C2F, K4] 3 times, C2B, K2, C2F*, K1, m1r, sm, K2, m1l; rpt from * to * once, K1, m1r, K1. (84 sts)

Rnd 39: Knit.

Rnd 40: K2, [C2B, K4, C2F, K2] 8 times, K2.

Rnd 41: Knit.

Rnd 42: *K1, [C2B, K6, C2F] 4 times, K1; rpt from * once more.

Rnd 43: Knit.

Rnd 44: *[C2B, K8] 4 times, C2F; rpt from * once more.

Change to a 3mm circular needle.

Rnd 45: K19, K2tog, K40, K2tog, K21. (82 sts)

Rnd 46: Purl.

Rnd 47: Knit.

Rnd 48: Purl.

Cast off.

SLEEVES

Starting at under arm, slip the 26 sts held on waste yarn for one sleeve evenly onto three 3.5mm dpns and rejoin yarn.

Using fourth dpn, start knitting in the round.

Rnd 1: Knit.

Rnd 2: [K6, C2B, C2F] twice, K6.

Rnd 3: Knit.

Rnd 4: K1, m1l, [K4, C2B, K2, C2F] twice, K4, m1r, K1. (28 sts)

Rnd 5: Knit.

Rnd 6: K1, [C2F, K2, C2B, K4] twice, C2F, K2, C2B, K1.

Rnd 7: Knit.

Rnd 8: K2, [C2F, C2B, K6] twice, C2F, C2B, K2.

Rnd 9: Knit.

Rnd 10: K3, [C2B, K8] twice, C2B, K3.

Rnd 11: Knit.

Rnd 12: K1, m1l, K1, [C2B, C2F, K6] twice, C2B, C2F, K1, m1r, K1. (30 sts)

Rnd 13: Knit.

Rnd 14: [K2, C2B, K2, C2F, K2] 3 times.

Rnd 15: Knit.

Rnd 16: [K1, C2B, K4, C2F, K1] 3 times.

Rnd 17: Knit.

Rnd 18: [C2B, K6, C2F] 3 times.

Rnd 19: Knit.

Rnd 20: K9, [C2B, K8] twice, K1.

Change to a set of 3mm dpns.

Rnd 21: K14, K2tog, K14. (29 sts)

Rnd 22: Purl.

Rnd 23: Knit.

Rnd 24: Purl.

Cast off.

Repeat for second sleeve.

MAKING UP

1. If necessary, close hole under arm with a couple of stitches.

2. Block the sweater.

3. Sew buttons in place on left-hand button band, matching them up with the buttonholes.

STRIPED SHORTS

The shorts are worked top down with no seams. The top part is worked back and forth with a button band opening at the back and some short row shaping for the bottom; the lower half and legs are worked in the round. The button band is worked in Yarn B throughout using the Intarsia method (see Techniques: Colourwork).

Using 3mm straight needles and Yarn B, cast on 52 sts.

Row 1 (ws): Knit.

Row 2: Knit.

Row 3 (buttonhole row): Knit to last 3 sts, K2tog, YO, K1.

Rows 4–5: Knit 2 rows.

Change to 3.5mm straight needles.

Row 6: [K1, K1fb] 11 times, K1fb 3 times, K1, K1fb 4 times, [K1, K1fb] 10 times, K2. (80 sts)

Row 7: K2, P8, turn.

Row 8: YO, knit to end.

Row 9: (B) K2, (C) P8, SSP, P2, turn.

Row 10: (C) YO, knit to last 2 sts, (B) K2.

Row 11: (B) K2, P11, SSP, P2, turn.

Row 12: (B) YO, knit to end.

Row 13: (B) K2, (C) P14, SSP, P2, turn.

Row 14: (C) YO, knit to last 2 sts, (B) K2.

Row 15: (B) K2, P17, SSP, purl to last 2 sts, K2.

Row 16: (B) K10, turn.

Row 17: (B) YO, purl to last 2 sts, K2.

Row 18: (B) K2, (C) K8, K2tog, K2, turn.

Row 19 (buttonhole row): (C) YO, purl to last 3 sts, P2tog, (B) YO, K1.

Row 20: (B) K13, K2tog, K2, turn.

Row 21: (B) YO, purl to last 2 sts, K2.

Row 22: (B) K2, (C) K14, K2tog, K2, turn.

Row 23: (C) YO, purl to last 2 sts, (B) K2.

Row 24: (B) K19, K2tog, knit to end.

Row 25: (B) K2, purl to last 2 sts, K2.

Row 26: (B) K2, (C) knit to last 2 sts, (B) K2.

Row 27 (buttonhole row): (B) K2, (C) purl to last 3 sts, P2tog, (B) YO, K1.

Row 28: (B) Knit.

Row 29: (B) K2, purl to last 2 sts, K2.

Row 30: (B) K2, (C) knit to last 2 sts, (B) K2.

Row 31: (B) K2, (C) purl to last 2 sts, (B) K2.

From this point the shorts are worked in a stripe pattern of 2 rows Yarn B and 2 rows Yarn C, beginning with Yarn B and without the button band.

Row 32: Transfer sts to a 3.5mm circular needle and knit to last 2 sts, slip the last 2 sts (without working them) onto a cable needle.

Join to work in the round:

Rnd 33: Position the cable needle behind the first 2 sts on the LH needle, knit first st on LH needle together with first st on cable needle, place marker for beginning of round, knit next st on LH needle together with remaining st on cable needle, knit to end. (78 sts)

Rnds 34–37: Knit 4 rnds.

Rnd 38: K1, m1l, knit to last st, m1r, K1. (80 sts)

Rnds 39–40: Knit 2 rnds.

Rnd 41: K1, m1l, knit to last st, m1r, K1. (82 sts)

Rnd 42: K40, m1r, K2, m1l, knit to end. (84 sts)

Rnd 43: K1, m1l, knit to last st, m1r, K1. (86 sts)

Rnd 44: Knit.

Rnd 45: K1, m1l, K41, m1r, K2, m1l, K41, m1r, K1. (90 sts)

Rnd 46: Knit.

Rnd 47: K1, m1l, K43, m1r, K2, m1l, K43, m1r, K1. (94 sts)

Rnd 48: Knit.

Divide for legs:

Rnd 49: K47 (right leg), without working them place next 47 sts onto waste yarn (left leg).

RIGHT LEG

Rnds 50–53: Knit 4 rnds.

Rnd 54: SSK, K22, K2tog, knit to end. (45 sts)

Rnds 55–57: Knit 3 rnds.

Rnd 58: SSK, K20, K2tog, knit to end. (43 sts)

Rnds 59–61: Knit 3 rnds.

Rnd 62: SSK, K18, K2tog, knit to end. (41 sts)

Rnd 63: Knit.

Change to 3mm circular needle and continue in Yarn B only.

Rnd 64: Knit.

Rnd 65: Purl.

Rnds 66–67: Rpt last 2 rnds once more.

LEFT LEG

Rnd 49: Transfer sts from waste yarn to 3.5mm circular needle, place marker for beginning of round and rejoin Yarn B, knit 1 rnd.

Continue working the stripe pattern of 2 rows Yarn B and 2 rows Yarn C, beginning with Yarn C.

Rnds 50–53: Knit 4 rnds.

Rnd 54: K21, SSK, K22, K2tog. (45 sts)

Rnds 55–57: Knit 3 rnds.

Rnd 58: K21, SSK, K20, K2tog. (43 sts)

Rnds 59–61: Knit 3 rnds.

Rnd 62: K21, SSK, K18, K2tog. (41 sts)

Rnd 63: Knit.

Change to 3mm circular needle and continue in Yarn B only.

Rnd 64: Knit.

Rnd 65: Purl.

Rnds 66–67: Rpt last 2 rnds once more.

Cast off.

MAKING UP

1. If necessary, close hole where the 2 legs join with a couple of stitches.

2. Block the shorts.

3. Sew buttons in place on left-hand button band down back of shorts, matching them up with the buttonholes.

SNEAKERS

Using 2.75mm needles and Yarn C for the soles, follow the pattern for the Sneakers (see Shoes and Accessories), changing to Yarn A for the upper parts of the shoes. Make the laces with Yarn C.

TILLY
THE HARE

A cardigan with a carrot motif seems like
the perfect choice for an afternoon at the
allotment, but Tilly's beautiful white dress
is unlikely to stay that way for long...

YOU WILL NEED

FOR TILLY'S BODY

• Scheepjes Stonewashed
(50g/130m; 78% cotton/22%
acrylic) yarn in the
following shades:

  - *Yarn A Ecru (Axinite 831),
    2 balls*

  - *Yarn B Cream (Moonstone
    801), 1 ball*

• 2.75mm (US 2) straight needles

• Toy stuffing

• 2 x 10mm (½in) buttons

• Scrap piece of 4-ply yarn
for embroidering nose

• 35mm (1⅜in) pompom maker

• FOR TILLY'S OUTFIT

• Scheepjes Catona (10g/25m,
25g/62m or 50g/125m;
100% cotton) yarn in the
following shades:

  - *Yarn A Cream (Old Lace 130),
    1 x 50g ball and 1 x 25g ball*

  - *Yarn B Pale Grey (Light Silver
    172), 1 x 50g ball*

  - *Yarn C Peach (Rich Coral 410),
    1 x 10g ball*

  - *Yarn D Orange (Royal Orange
    189), 1 x 10g ball*

  - *Yarn E Green (Lime 512),
    1 x 10g ball*

• 3mm (US 2½) straight needles

• 3mm (US 2½) circular
needle (23cm/9in length)

• Set of four 3mm (US 2½)
double-pointed needles

• 3.5mm (US 4) straight needles

• 3.5mm (US 4) circular
needle (23cm/9in length)

• Set of four 3.5mm (US 4)
double-pointed needles

• Cable needle

• Waste yarn

• 10 small buttons

Before you start, please read the Essential Notes at the beginning of this book.

HARE PATTERN

HEAD

Starting at neck:

Using 2.75mm straight needles and Yarn A, cast on 11 sts.

Row 1 (ws): Purl.

Row 2: [K1, M1] to last st, K1. (21 sts)

Row 3: Purl.

Row 4: [K2, M1] to last st, K1. (31 sts)

Row 5: Purl.

Row 6: K1, m1l, knit to last st, m1r, K1. (33 sts)

Row 7: Purl.

Row 8: [K1, m1l, K15, m1r] twice, K1. (37 sts)

Row 9: Purl.

Row 10: [K1, m1l, K17, m1r] twice, K1. (41 sts)

Row 11: P20, m1pl, P1, m1pr, P20. (43 sts)

Row 12: [K1, m1l, K20, m1r] twice, K1. (47 sts)

Row 13: P23, m1pl, P1, m1pr, P23. (49 sts)

Row 14: K24, m1r, K1, m1l, K24. (51 sts)

Row 15: Purl.

Row 16: [K1, m1l, K24, m1r] twice, K1. (55 sts)

Row 17: Purl.

Row 18: K27, sl1, K27.

Rows 19–21: Rpt last 2 rows once more, then rpt Row 17 again.

Row 22: K26, CDD, K26. (53 sts)

Row 23: Purl.

Row 24: K25, CDD, K25. (51 sts)

Row 25: P24, PCDD, P24. (49 sts)

Row 26: K23, CDD, K23. (47 sts)

Row 27: Purl.

Row 28: K1, K2tog, K19, CDD, K19, SSK, K1. (43 sts)

Row 29: Purl.

Row 30: K20, CDD, K20. (41 sts)

Row 31: Purl.

Row 32: K1, K2tog, K17, sl1, K17, SSK, K1. (39 sts)

Row 33: Purl.

Row 34: K19, sl1, K19.

Row 35: Purl.

Row 36: K1, K2tog, K16, sl1, K16, SSK, K1. (37 sts)

Row 37: Purl.

Row 38: K18, sl1, K18.

Row 39: Purl.

Row 40: K1, K2tog, K3, K2tog 4 times, K3, CDD, K3, SSK 4 times, K3, SSK, K1. (25 sts)

Row 41: Purl.

Row 42: K1, K2tog 5 times, CDD, SSK 5 times, K1. (13 sts)

Row 43: Purl.

Cast off.

EARS (MAKE 2)

Using 2.75mm straight needles and Yarn A, cast on 15 sts.

Row 1 (ws): (A) P6, (B) P3, (A) P6.

Row 2: (A) K6, (B) [K1, M1] 3 times, (A) K6. (18 sts)

Row 3: (A) P6, (B) P6, (A) P6.

Row 4: (A) K6, (B) K6, (A) K6.

Row 5: (A) P6, (B) P6, (A) P6.

Row 6: (A) K4, m1r, K2, (B) K1, m1l, K4, m1r, K1, (A) K2, m1l, K4. (22 sts)

Row 7: (A) P7, (B) P8, (A) P7.

Row 8: (A) K7, (B) K8, (A) K7.

Row 9: (A) P7, (B) P8, (A) P7.

Row 10: (A) K5, m1r, K2, (B) K1, m1l, K6, m1r, K1, (A) K2, m1l, K5. (26 sts)

Row 11: (A) P8, (B) P10, (A) P8.

Row 12: (A) K8, (B) K10, (A) K8.

Rows 13–15: Rpt last 2 rows once more, then rpt Row 11 again.

Row 16: (A) K6, m1r, K2, (B) K1, m1l, K8, m1r, K1, (A) K2, m1l, K6. (30 sts)

Row 17: (A) P9, (B) P12, (A) P9.

Row 18: (A) K9, (B) K12, (A) K9.

Rows 19–27: Rpt last 2 rows 4 more times, then rpt Row 17 again.

Row 28: (A) K6, K2tog, K1, (B) SSK, K8, K2tog, (A) K1, SSK, K6. (26 sts)

Row 29: (A) P8, (B) P10, (A) P8.

Row 30: (A) K8, (B) K10, (A) K8.

Row 31: (A) P8, (B) P10, (A) P8.

Row 32: (A) K5, K2tog, K1, (B) SSK, K6, K2tog, (A) K1, SSK, K5. (22 sts)

Rows 33–35: Rpt Rows 7–9.

Row 36: (A) K4, K2tog, K1, (B) SSK, K4, K2tog, (A) K1, SSK, K4. (18 sts)

Rows 37–39: Rpt Rows 3–5.

Row 40: (A) K3, K2tog, K1, (B) SSK, K2, K2tog, (A) K1, SSK, K3. (14 sts)

Row 41: (A) P5, (B) P4, (A) P5.

Row 42: (A) K2, K2tog, K1, (B) SSK, K2tog, (A) K1, SSK, K2. (10 sts)

Row 43: (A) P4, (B) P2, (A) P4.

Cut Yarn B leaving a long tail and continue in Yarn A.

Row 44: K1, [K2tog, SSK] twice, K1. (6 sts)

Row 45: Purl.

Cut yarn leaving a long tail. Using a tapestry needle, thread tail through the stitches left on needle and pull up tight to gather stitches.

TAIL

Using Yarn B make a pompom approximately 35mm (1⅜in) diameter.

BODY

Work as Standard Body – Plain (see Standard Body Parts).

ARMS (MAKE 2)

Work as Standard Arms (see Standard Body Parts).

LEGS (MAKE 2)

Work as Standard Legs – Contrast Foot Pad (see Standard Body Parts).

MAKING UP

Follow the instructions in the techniques section (see Techniques: Making Up Your Animal).

OUTFIT PATTERNS

DRESS

The dress is worked top down, seamlessly with raglan cap sleeves. The top half is worked back and forth with a button band down the back and the bottom half is worked in the round.

To K1 under loose strand, insert RH needle under loose strand from 2 rows below and knit next stitch, bringing the stitch under the strand and out toward you (photo 1).

Using 3mm straight needles and Yarn A, cast on 31 sts.

Row 1 (ws): Knit.

Row 2 (buttonhole row): K1, YO, K2tog, knit to end.

Change to 3.5mm straight needles.

Row 3: K3, P4, pm, P4, pm, P10, pm, P4, pm, knit to last 3 sts, K3.

Row 4: [Knit to marker, m1r, sm, K1, m1l] twice, K2, sl5wyif, [knit to marker, m1r, sm, K1, m1l] twice, knit to end. (39 sts)

Row 5: K3, purl to last 3 sts, K3.

Row 6: [Knit to marker, m1r, sm, K1, m1l] twice, K5, K1 under loose strand, [knit to marker, m1r, sm, K1, m1l] twice, knit to end. (47 sts)

Row 7: As Row 5.

Row 8: [Knit to marker, m1r, sm, K1, m1l] twice, [K1, sl5wyif] twice, K1, [knit to marker, m1r, sm, K1, m1l] twice, knit to end. (55 sts)

Row 9: As Row 5.

Row 10: [Knit to marker, m1r, sm, K1, m1l] twice, [K4, K1 under loose strand, K1] twice, [knit to marker, m1r, sm, K1, m1l] twice, knit to end. (63 sts)

1

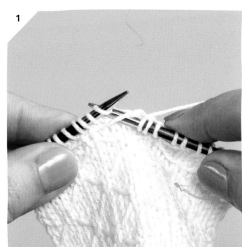

Row 11: As Row 5.

Row 12: [Knit to marker, m1r, sm, K1, m1l] twice, [sl5wyif, K1] twice, sl5wyif, [knit to marker, m1r, sm, K1, m1l] twice, knit to end. (71 sts)

Row 13: As Row 5.

Row 14: [Knit to marker, m1r, sm, K1, m1l] twice, [K3, K1 under loose strand, K2] 3 times, [knit to marker, m1r, sm, K1, m1l] twice, knit to end. (79 sts)

Row 15: As Row 5.

Row 16 (buttonhole row): K1, YO, K2tog, [knit to marker, m1r, sm, K1, m1l] twice, [sl4wyif, K1, sl1wyif] 3 times, sl3wyif, [knit to marker, m1r, sm, K1, m1l] twice, knit to end. (87 sts)

Row 17: As Row 5.

Row 18: [Knit to marker, m1r, sm, K1, m1l] twice, [K2, K1 under loose strand, K3] 3 times, K2, K1 under loose strand, [knit to marker, m1r, sm, K1, m1l] twice, knit to end. (95 sts)

Row 19: As Row 5.

Row 20: [Knit to marker, m1r, sm, K1, m1l] twice, [sl3wyif, K1, sl2wyif] 4 times, sl1wyif, [knit to marker, m1r, sm, K1, m1l] twice, knit to end. (103 sts)

Row 21: As Row 5.

Row 22: [Knit to marker, m1r, sm, K1, m1l] twice, [K1, K1 under loose strand, K4] 4 times, K1, K1 under loose strand, [knit to marker, m1r, sm, K1, m1l] twice, knit to end. (111 sts)

Row 23: As Row 5.

Row 24: [Knit to marker, m1r, sm, K1, m1l] twice, [sl2wyif, K1, sl3wyif] 4 times, sl2wyif, K1, sl2wyif, [knit to marker, m1r, sm, K1, m1l] twice, knit to end. (119 sts)

Row 25: K3, *purl to marker, remove marker (left back), cast off 25 sts (sleeve), P1, sm; rpt from * once more (front and sleeve), purl to last 3 sts, K3 (right back). (69 sts)

Row 26: Knit to marker, sm, K1, m1a, K1, K1 under loose strand, [K5, K1 under loose strand] 5 times, sm, K1, m1a, knit to end. (71 sts)

Row 27: As Row 5.

Change to 3mm straight needles and Yarn C.

Row 28: [Knit to marker, m1r, sm, K3, m1l] twice, knit to end. (75 sts)

Row 29: Knit.

Change to 3.5mm straight needles and Yarn A.

Row 30 (buttonhole row): K1, YO, K2tog, knit to end.

Row 31: As Row 5.

Row 32: Knit to marker, m1r, sm, K3, m1l, K13, [K1fb] 6 times, knit to marker, m1r, sm, K3, m1l, knit to end. (85 sts)

Row 33: As Row 5.

Row 34: Knit.

Row 35: As Row 5.

Row 36: [Knit to marker, m1r, sm, K3, m1l] twice, knit to end. (89 sts)

Rows 37–41: Rpt Rows 33–36 once more, then rpt Row 33 again. (93 sts)

Row 42 (buttonhole row): As Row 30.

Rows 43–44: Rpt Rows 35–36. (97 sts)

Row 45–51: Rpt Rows 33–36, then rpt Rows 33–35 once more. (101 sts)

Rows 52–53: Rpt Rows 34–35.

Row 54: Transfer sts to a 3.5mm circular needle, [knit to marker, m1r, sm, K3, m1l] twice, knit to last 3 sts, slip the last 3 sts (without working them) onto a cable needle. (105 sts)

Join to work in the round:

Rnd 55: Position cable needle behind first 3 sts on LH needle, place marker for beginning of round, knit first st on LH needle together with first st on cable needle, rpt for next 2 sts, knit to end. (102 sts)

Rnd 56–57: Knit 2 rnds.

Rnd 58: K1, [K1 sl5wyif] to last 5 sts, K1, sl4wyif.

Rnd 59: Sl1wyif, knit to end.

Rnd 60: K4, [K1 under loose strand, K5] to last 2 sts, K1 under loose strand, K1.

Rnd 61: Knit to last st, sl1wyif.

Rnd 62: Sl4wyif, K1, [sl5wyif, K1] to last st, K1.

Rnd 63: Knit.

Rnd 64: K1, [K1 under loose strand, K5] to last 5 sts, K1 under loose strand, K4.

Rnd 65: Knit.

Rnds 66–80: Rpt Rnds 58–65 once more, then rpt Rnds 58–64 again.

Change to 3mm circular needle.

Rnd 81: Knit.

Rnd 82: Purl.

Cast off.

MAKING UP

1. Block dress.

2. Sew buttons in place on LH button band down back of dress, matching them up with the buttonholes.

CARDIGAN

The cardigan is worked top down, seamlessly and with a round Fair Isle yoke. The body is worked back and forth in rows and the sleeves are worked in the round. The button bands (first and last 3 sts of each row) are worked in Yarn B throughout using the Intarsia method (see Techniques: Colourwork).

Using Yarn B and 3mm straight needles, cast on 39 sts.

Row 1 (ws): Knit.

Row 2 (buttonhole row): K1, YO, K2tog, knit to end.

Row 3: Knit.

Change to 3.5mm straight needles.

Row 4: K4, [K1, K1fb] to last 3 sts, K3. (55 sts)

Row 5: K3, purl to last 3 sts, K3.

Carrot Chart is worked over the next 14 rows, in stocking stitch and using Fair Isle (Stranded) technique (see Techniques: Colourwork). The chart is repeated across the rows 16 times and then column 1 is worked once more. Read RS rows from

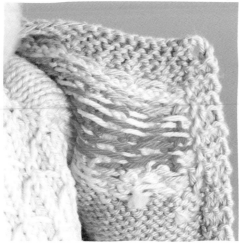

right to left and WS rows from left to right. The button bands (first and last 3 sts of each row) are worked in Yarn B using the Intarsia method (see Techniques: Colourwork).

Rows 6–9: K3, work Carrot Chart to last 3 sts, K3. (71 sts)

Row 10 (buttonhole row): K1, YO, K2tog, work Carrot Chart to last 3 sts, K3.

Rows 11–17: K3, work Carrot Chart to last 3 sts, K3. (103 sts)

Row 18 (buttonhole row): K1, YO, K2tog, work Carrot Chart to last 3 sts, K3.

Row 19: K3, work Carrot Chart to last 3 sts, K3.

Row 20: (B) K3, (A) [K6, M1] to last 4 sts, K1, (B) K3. (119 sts)

Continue in Yarn B.

Row 21: K3, purl to last 3 sts, K3.

Row 22: Knit.

Row 23: As Row 21.

Row 24: K18 (left front), without working them place next 25 sts onto waste yarn (sleeve), K33 (back), without working them place next 25 sts onto waste yarn (sleeve), knit to end (right front). (69 sts)

Row 25: K3, P16, pm, P33, pm, purl to last 3 sts, K3.

Row 26 (buttonhole row): K1, YO, K2tog, [knit to marker, m1r, sm, K2, m1l] twice, knit to end. (73 sts)

Row 27: K3, purl to last 3 sts, K3.

Row 28: Knit.

Row 29: As Row 27.

Row 30: [Knit to marker, m1r, sm, K2, m1l] twice, knit to end. (77 sts)

Rows 31–33: Rpt Rows 27–29.

Row 34 (buttonhole row): K1, YO, K2tog, [knit to marker, m1r, sm, K2, m1l] twice, knit to end. (81 sts)

Rows 35–40: Rpt Rows 27–30, then rpt Rows 27–28 again. (85 sts)

Change to 3mm straight needles.

Row 41: Knit.

Row 42 (buttonhole row): K1, YO, K2tog, knit to end.

Row 43: Knit.

Cast off.

SLEEVES

Starting at under arm, slip the 25 sts held on waste yarn for one sleeve evenly onto three 3.5mm dpns and rejoin yarn.

Using fourth dpn start knitting in the round.

Rnds 1–3: Knit 3 rnds.

Rnd 4: K1, m1l, knit to last st, m1r, K1. (27 sts)

Rnds 5–11: Knit 7 rnds.

Rnd 12: K1, m1l, knit to last st, m1r, K1. (29 sts)

Rnds 13–20: Knit 8 rnds.

Change to a set of 3mm dpns.

Rnd 21: Knit.

Rnd 22: Purl.

Rnds 23–24: Rpt last 2 rnds once more.

Cast off.

Repeat for second sleeve.

MAKING UP

1. Block the cardigan.

2. Sew buttons in place on front right-hand button band, matching them up with the buttonholes.

FRENCH KNICKERS

Using Yarn A, follow the pattern for the French Knickers (see Shoes and Accessories).

CARROT CHART

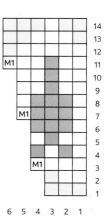

KEY

☐ Yarn A

☐ Yarn B

▨ Yarn D

■ Yarn E

M1 Make 1

AMELIA
THE DUCK

When she's in a hurry, Amelia saves time by simply slipping into her stylish shift dress with its little button tab, and grabbing her shoulder bag. She's ready in a jiffy and won't miss her train after all!

YOU WILL NEED

FOR AMELIA'S BODY
• Scheepjes Stonewashed (50g/130m; 78% cotton/22% acrylic) yarn in the following shades:

 - *Yarn A* Cream (Moonstone 801), 2 balls

 - *Yarn B* Orange (Coral 816), 1 ball

• 2.75mm (US 2) straight needles

• Toy stuffing

• 2 x 10mm (½in) buttons

FOR AMELIA'S OUTFIT
• Scheepjes Catona (10g/25m, 25g/62m or 50g/125m; 100% cotton) yarn in the following shades:

 - *Yarn A* Light Blue (Bluebell 173), 1 x 50g ball

 - *Yarn B* Dark Blue (Light Navy 164), 1 x 50g ball

 - *Yarn C* Orange (Rich Coral 410), 1 x 10g ball

 - *Yarn D* Peach (Vintage Peach 414), 1 x 25g ball

• 3mm (US 2½) straight needles

• 3mm (US 2½) circular needle (23cm/9in length)

• Set of four 3mm (US 2½) double-pointed needles

• 3.5mm (US 4) straight needles

• 3.5mm (US 4) circular needle (23cm/9in length)

• Set of four 3.5mm (US 4) double-pointed needles

• Cable needle

• Waste yarn

• 9 small buttons

Before you start, please read the Essential Notes at the beginning of this book.

DUCK PATTERN

HEAD

Starting at neck:

Using 2.75mm straight needles and Yarn A, cast on 11 sts.

Row 1 (ws): Purl.

Row 2: [K1, M1] to last st, K1. (21 sts)

Row 3: Purl.

Row 4: [K2, M1] to last st, K1. (31 sts)

Row 5: Purl.

Row 6: K1, m1l, knit to last st, m1r, K1. (33 sts)

Row 7: Purl.

Row 8: [K1, m1l, K15, m1r] twice, K1. (37 sts)

Row 9: Purl.

Row 10: [K1, m1l, K17, m1r] twice, K1. (41 sts)

Row 11: P20, P1 and place a removable marker around this stitch on RS, P20.

Row 12: [K1, m1l, K19, m1r] twice, K1. (45 sts)

Row 13: Purl.

Row 14: K22, m1r, K1, m1l, K22. (47 sts)

Row 15: Purl.

Row 16: K1, m1l, knit to last st, m1r, K1. (49 sts)

Row 17: Purl.

Row 18: K18, *K1 and place a removable marker around this stitch*, K11; rpt from * to *, K18.

Rows 19–25: Stocking stitch 7 rows.

Row 26: K23, CDD, K23. (47 sts)

Row 27: Purl.

Row 28: K1, K2tog, K19, CDD, K19, SSK, K1. (43 sts)

Row 29: Purl.

Row 30: K20, CDD, K20. (41 sts)

Row 31: P20, P1 and place a removable marker around this stitch on RS, P20.

Row 32: K1, K2tog, K17, sl1, K17, SSK, K1. (39 sts)

Row 33: Purl.

Row 34: K19, sl1, K19.

Row 35: Purl.

Row 36: K1, K2tog, K16, sl1, K16, SSK, K1. (37 sts)

Row 37: Purl.

Row 38: K18, sl1, K18.

Row 39: Purl.

Row 40: K1, K2tog, K3, K2tog 4 times, K3, CDD, K3, SSK 4 times, K3, SSK, K1. (25 sts)

Row 41: Purl.

Row 42: K1, K2tog 5 times, CDD, SSK 5 times, K1. (13 sts)

Row 43: Purl.

Cast off.

BEAK

Using 2.75mm straight needles and Yarn B, cast on 33 sts.

Row 1 (ws): Purl.

Row 2: K6, sl1, K8, CDD, K8, sl1, K6. (31 sts)

Row 3: Purl.

Row 4: K6, sl1, K7, CDD, K7, sl1, K6. (29 sts)

Row 5: Purl.

Row 6: K6, sl1, K15, sl1, K6.

Rows 7–19: Rpt last 2 rows 6 more times, then rpt Row 5 again.

Row 20: K5, CDD, K13, CDD, K5. (25 sts)

Row 21: Purl.

Row 22: K4, CDD, K11, CDD, K4. (21 sts)

Row 23: P3, PCDD, P9, PCDD, P3. (17 sts)

Row 24: K2, CDD, K7, CDD, K2. (13 sts)

Cut yarn leaving a long tail. Using a tapestry needle, thread tail through the stitches left on needle and pull up tight to gather stitches.

TAIL

Using 2.75mm straight needles and Yarn A, cast on 27 sts.

Row 1 (ws): P18, turn.

Row 2: YO, K9, turn.

Row 3: YO, P9, SSP, P1, turn.

Row 4: YO, K11, K2tog, K1, turn.

Row 5: YO, P13, SSP, P1, turn.

Row 6: YO, K15, K2tog, K1, turn.

Row 7: YO, P17, SSP, P1, turn.

Row 8: YO, K19, K2tog, K1, turn.

Row 9: YO, P21, SSP, purl to end.

Row 10: K24, K2tog, knit to end.

Rows 11–13: Stocking stitch 3 rows.

Row 14: K1, K2tog, K21, SSK, K1. (25 sts)

Row 15: Purl.

Row 16: [K1, K2tog, K7, SSK] twice, K1. (21 sts)

Row 17: Purl.

Row 18: K1, K2tog, K15, SSK, K1. (19 sts)

Row 19: Purl.

Row 20: [K1, K2tog, K4, SSK] twice, K1. (15 sts)

Row 21: Purl.

Row 22: [K1, K2tog, K2, SSK] twice, K1. (11 sts)

Row 23: Purl.

Row 24: K1, K2tog, K1, CDD, K1, SSK, K1. (7 sts)

Rows 25–28: Stocking stitch 4 rows.

Cut yarn leaving a long tail. Using a tapestry needle, thread tail through the stitches left on needle and pull up tight to gather stitches.

BODY

Work as Standard Body – Plain (see Standard Body Parts).

ARMS (MAKE 2)

Work as Standard Arms (see Standard Body Parts).

LEGS (MAKE 2)

Work as Standard Leg – Contrast Foot Pad (see Standard Body Parts).

MAKING UP

Follow the instructions in the techniques section (see Techniques: Making Up Your Animal).

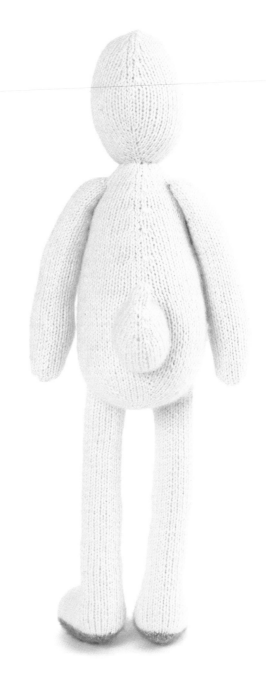

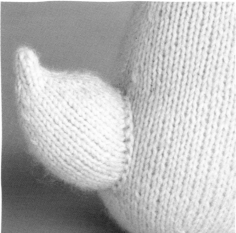

OUTFIT PATTERNS

STRIPED DRESS

The dress is worked top down, seamlessly with raglan sleeves. The top half is worked back and forth in rows with a button band opening at the back, the bottom half and the sleeves are worked in the round. The button band is worked in Yarn B throughout using the Intarsia method (see Techniques: Colourwork).

Using 3mm straight needles and Yarn C, cast on 31 sts.

Row 1 (ws): Knit.

Row 2 (buttonhole row): K1, YO, K2tog, knit to end.

Row 3: Knit.

Row 4: K3, [K1, K1fb, K1] to last 4 sts, K4. (39 sts)

Change to 3.5mm straight needles and Yarn A.

The dress is now worked in a stripe pattern of 2 rows Yarn A and 2 rows Yarn B. The button bands (first and last 3 sts on each row) are worked in Yarn A throughout, using the Intarsia method (see Techniques: Colourwork).

Row 5: K3, P5, pm, P6, pm, P12, pm, P6, pm, P4, K3.

Row 6: [Knit to marker, m1r, sm, K1, m1l] 4 times, knit to end. (47 sts)

Row 7: (A) K3, (B) purl to last 3 sts, (A) K3.

Row 8: (A) K3, (B) [knit to marker, m1r, sm, K1, m1l] 4 times, knit to last 3 sts, (A) K3. (55 sts)

Row 9: K3, purl to last 3 sts, K3.

Row 10: As Row 6. (63 sts)

Rows 11–15: Rpt Rows 7–10 once more, then rpt Row 7 again. (79 sts)

Row 16 (buttonhole row): (A) K1, YO, K2tog, (B) [knit to marker, m1r, sm, K1, m1l] 4 times, knit to last 3 sts, (A) K3. (87 sts)

Rows 17–23: Rpt Rows 9–15. (111 sts)

Row 24: As Row 8. (119 sts)

Row 25: K3, *purl to marker, remove marker (left back), without working them place next 25 sts onto waste yarn (sleeve), P1, sm; rpt from * once more (front and sleeve), purl to last 3 sts, K3 (right back). (69 sts)

Row 26: K31, K1fb 6 times, knit to end. (75 sts)

Row 27: (A) K3, (B) purl to last 3 sts, (A) K3.

Row 28: (A) K3, (B) [knit to marker, m1r, sm, K2, m1l] twice, knit to last 3 sts, (A) K3. (79 sts)

Row 29: K3, purl to last 3 sts, K3.

Row 30 (buttonhole row): K1, YO, K2tog, knit to end.

Row 31: As Row 27.

Row 32: As Row 28. (83 sts)

Row 33: As Row 29.

Row 34: Knit.

Rows 35–38: Rpt Rows 31–34 once more. (87 sts)

Rows 39–42: Rpt Rows 27–30. (91 sts)

Rows 43–50: Rpt Rows 31–34 twice. (99 sts)

Row 51: As Row 27.

Row 52: (A) K3, (B) knit to last 3 sts, (A) K3.

Row 53: As Row 29.

Row 54: Transfer sts to a 3.5mm circular needle, [knit to marker, m1r, sm, K2, m1l] twice, knit to last 3 sts, slip the last 3 sts (without working them) onto a cable needle. (103 sts)

Join to work in the round:

Continue working in stripe pattern of 2 rows Yarn A and 2 rows Yarn B.

Rnd 55: Position cable needle behind first 3 sts on LH needle, place marker for beginning of round, knit first st on LH needle together with first st on cable needle, rpt for next 2 sts, knit to end. (100 sts)

Rnd 56–74: Knit 19 rnds.

Change to 3mm circular needle and Yarn C.

Rnd 75: [K3, K2tog] to end. (80 sts)

Rnd 76: Purl.

Rnd 77: Knit.

Rnds 78–79: Rpt last 2 rnds once more.

Cast off.

SLEEVES

Starting at under arm, slip the 25 sts held on waste yarn for one sleeve evenly onto three 3.5mm dpns and rejoin yarn.

Using fourth dpn start knitting in the round.

The sleeves are worked in a stripe rpt of 2 rows Yarn A and 2 rows Yarn B, starting with Yarn A.

Rnds 1–3: Knit 3 rnds.

Rnd 4: K1, m1l, knit to last st, m1r, K1. (27 sts)

Rnds 5–11: Knit 7 rnds.

Rnd 12: K1, m1l, knit to last st, m1r, K1. (29 sts)

Rnds 13–14: Knit 2 rnds.

Change to a set of 3mm dpns and Yarn C.

Rnd 15: Knit.

Rnd 16: Purl.

Rnds 17–18: Rpt last 2 rnds once more.

Cast off.

Repeat for second sleeve.

BUTTON TAB

Using 3mm straight needles and Yarn C, cast on 5 sts.

Row 1 (ws): Knit.

Row 2–23: Knit 23 rows.

Cast off.

MAKING UP

1. If necessary, close hole under arm with a couple of stitches.

2. Block dress.

3. With wrong sides facing, sew the cast-off end of the button tab to the inside of the bottom of the dress just under the 2nd pale blue stripe up from the hem.

4. Fold the button tab over the hem and to the front of the dress, sew button in place, sewing through the button tab and dress.

5. Sew buttons in place on left-hand button band down back of dress, matching them up with the buttonholes.

SHOPPER BAG

The bag is worked in one piece and seamed at the side and bottom, with an i-cord strap.

BAG

Using 3mm straight needles and Yarn D, cast on 36 sts.

Row 1 (ws): Knit.

Row 2: [K1fb, K15, K1fb, K1] twice. (40 sts)

Row 3: Knit.

Row 4: [K1, K1fb, K15, K1fb, K2] twice. (44 sts)

Row 5: [K3, P4, K1, P6, K1, P4, K3] twice.

Row 6: [K2, P1, C4B, P1, C3B, C3F, P1, C4F, P1, K2] twice.

Row 7: As Row 5.

Row 8: [K2, P1, K4, P1, K6, P1, K4, P1, K2] twice.

Row 9: As Row 5.

Row 10: [K2, P1, C4B, P1, C3F, C3B, P1, C4F, P1, K2] twice.

Row 11: As Row 5.

Row 12: As Row 8.

Rows 13–19: Rpt Rows 5–11.

Row 20 (buttonhole row): K3, K2tog twice, K1, K3tog, YO, [K1, K2tog] twice, [K2tog , K2] twice, K2tog twice, [K1, K2tog, K1] twice, K2tog twice, K3. (31 sts)

Rows 21–25: Stocking stitch 5 rows.

Cast off.

STRAP

Using 3.5mm dpns and Yarn D, cast on 4 sts.

Make an i-cord, 85 rows (33cm/13in) long (see Techniques: Casting On and Stitches, Making i-cord).

MAKING UP

1. Block bag with the top edge rolled over slightly.

2. Sew up the side and bottom seam.

3. Sew a button in place on the back inside of bag, matching it up with the buttonhole.

4. Sew an end of the strap to the top of each side seam on the inside of the bag, slightly lower than the rolled-over edge.

FRENCH KNICKERS

Using Yarn D, follow the pattern for the French Knickers (see Shoes and Accessories).

HARRY
THE RAM

Harry's big sister has told him he must keep his best
sweater and new shorts clean, and she's lectured
him about not messing up his freshly combed fleece
or scuffing his smart shoes. Harry has other ideas.

YOU WILL NEED

FOR HARRY'S BODY
- Scheepjes Stonewashed (50g/130m; 78% cotton/22% acrylic) yarn in the following shades:

  - **Yarn A** Cream (Moonstone 801), 1 ball

  - **Yarn B** Ecru (Axinite 831), 2 balls

  - **Yarn C** Brown (Boulder Opal 804), 1 ball

- 2.75mm (US 2) straight needles

- Toy stuffing

- 2 x 10mm (½in) buttons

- Scrap piece of 4-ply yarn for embroidering nose

FOR HARRY'S OUTFIT
- Scheepjes Catona (10g/25m, 25g/62m or 50g/125m; 100% cotton) yarn in the following shades:

  - **Yarn A** Blue (Bluebird 247), 1 x 10g ball

  - **Yarn B** Cream (Old Lace 130), 1 x 50g ball

  - **Yarn C** Dark Blue (Light Navy 164), 1 x 50g ball

  - **Yarn D** Black (Jet Black 110), 1 x 10g ball

- 2.75mm (US 2) straight needles

- 3mm (US 2½) straight needles

- 3mm (US 2½) circular needle (23cm/9in length)

- Set of four 3mm (US 2½) double-pointed needles

- 3.5mm (US 4) straight needles

- 3.5mm (US 4) circular needle (23cm/9in length)

- Set of four 3.5mm (US 4) double-pointed needles

- Cable needle

- Waste yarn

- 10 small buttons

Before you start, please read the Essential Notes at the beginning of this book.

RAM PATTERN

For 'MB' (make bobble), cast on 2 sts using the Knit cast-on method (see Techniques: Casting On and Stitches), then knit 3 sts casting off the first 2 sts as you work them.

HEAD

Starting at neck:

Using 2.75mm straight needles and Yarn B, cast on 11 sts.

Row 1 (ws): Purl.

Row 2: [K1, M1] to last st, K1. (21 sts)

Row 3: Purl.

Row 4: [K2, M1] to last st, K1. (31 sts)

Row 5: (B) P14, (A) P3, (B) P14.

Row 6: (B) [MB, K1] 7 times, (A) K1, m1r, K1, m1l, K1, (B) [K1, MB] 6 times, K2. (33 sts)

Row 7: (B) P1, m1pr, P13, (A) P5, (B) P13, m1pl, P1. (35 sts)

Row 8: (B) [MB, K1] 7 times, (A) K3, m1r, K1, m1l, K3, (B) [K1, MB] 6 times, K2. (37 sts)

Row 9: (B) P1, m1pr, P13, (A) P4, m1pl, P1, m1pr, P4, (B) P13, m1pl, P1. (41 sts)

Row 10: (B) [MB, K1] 7 times, MB, (A) K5, m1r, K1, m1l, K5, (B) [MB, K1] 7 times, K1. (43 sts)

Row 11: (B) P1, m1pr, P13, (A) P7, m1pl, P1, m1pr, P7, (B) P13, m1pl, P1. (47 sts)

Row 12: (B) [MB, K1] 7 times, MB, (A) K8, m1r, K1, m1l, K8, (B) [MB, K1] 7 times, K1. (49 sts)

Row 13: (B) P1, m1pr, P14, (A) P9, m1pl, P1, m1pr, P9, (B) P14, m1pl, P1. (53 sts)

Row 14: (B) [MB, K1] 8 times, (A) K10, m1r, K1, m1l, K10, (B) [K1, MB] 7 times, K2. (55 sts)

Row 15: (B) P16, (A) P23, (B) P16.

Row 16: (B) [K1, MB] 8 times, (A) K11, m1r, K1, m1l, K11, (B) [MB, K1] 8 times. (57 sts)

Row 17: (B) P1, m1pr, P15, (A) P25, (B) P15, m1pl, P1. (59 sts)

Row 18: (B) [K1, MB] 8 times, (A) K13, sl1, K13, (B) [MB, K1] 8 times.

Row 19: (B) P16, (A) P27, (B) P16.

Row 20: (B) [MB, K1] 7 times, (A) K15, sl1, K15, (B) [K1, MB] 6 times, K2.

Row 21: (B) P14, (A) P31, (B) P14.

Row 22: (B) [K1, MB] 6 times, K1, (A) K16, sl1, K16, (B) [K1, MB] 6 times, K1.

Row 23: (B) P13, (A) P15, PCDD, P15, (B) P13. (57 sts)

Row 24: (B) [MB, K1] 6 times, MB, (A) K15, sl1, K15, (B) [MB, K1] 6 times, K1.

Row 25: (B) P13, (A) P14, PCDD, P14, (B) P13. (55 sts)

Row 26: (B) [K1, MB] 6 times, K1, (A) K13, CDD, K13, (B) [K1, MB] 6 times, K1. (53 sts)

Row 27: (B) P13, (A) P12, PCDD, P12, (B) P13. (51 sts)

Row 28: (B) [MB, K1] 6 times, MB, (A) K11, CDD, K11, (B) [MB, K1] 6 times, K1. (49 sts)

Row 29: (B) P1, SSP, P10, (A) P10, PCDD, P10, (B) P10, P2tog, P1. (45 sts)

Row 30: (B) [MB, K1] 6 times, (A) K9, CDD, K9, (B) [K1, MB] 5 times, K2. (43 sts)

Row 31: (B) P12, (A) P8, PCDD, P8, (B) P12. (41 sts)

Row 32: (B) [K1, MB] 6 times, K1, (A) K5, (B) [K1, MB] twice, K1, (A) K5, (B) [K1, MB] 6 times, K1.

Row 33: (B) P1, SSP, P10, (A) P4, (B) P7, (A) P4, (B) P10, P2tog, P1. (39 sts)

Continue in Yarn B only.

Row 34: [K1, MB] to last st, K1.

Row 35: Purl.

Row 36: [MB, K1] to last st, K1.

Row 37: P1, SSP, P33, P2tog, P1. (37 sts)

Row 38: [MB, K1] to last st, K1.

Row 39: Purl.

Row 40: [K1, MB] to last st, K1.

Row 41: P1, SSP, P3, SSP 4 times, P3, PCDD, P3, P2tog 4 times, P3, P2tog, P1. (25 sts)

Row 42: [K1, MB] to last st, K1.

Row 43: P1, SSP 5 times, PCDD, P2tog 5 times, P1. (13 sts)

Cast off.

EARS (MAKE 2)

Using 2.75mm straight needles and Yarn A, cast on 14 sts.

Row 1 (ws): Purl.

Row 2: K5, [K1, M1] 3 times, knit to end. (17 sts)

Rows 3–7: Stocking stitch 5 rows.

Row 8: [K3, K2tog, SSK] twice, K3. (13 sts)

Row 9: Purl.

Row 10: K1, [K1, K2tog, SSK] twice, K2. (9 sts)

Row 11: Purl.

Row 12: K1, K2tog, sl1 kw, K2tog, PSSO, SSK, K1. (5 sts)

Row 13: Purl.

Cut yarn leaving a long tail. Using a tapestry needle, thread tail through the stitches left on needle and pull up tight to gather stitches.

HORNS (MAKE 2)

Using 2.75mm straight needles and Yarn C, cast on 18 sts.

Row 1 (ws): P12, turn.

Row 2: YO, K6, turn.

Row 3: YO, P6, SSP, P1, turn.

Row 4: YO, K8, K2tog, K1, turn.

Row 5: YO, P10, SSP, P1, turn.

Row 6: YO, K12, K2tog, K1, turn.

Row 7: YO, P14, SSP, P to end.

Row 8: K16, K2tog, K1. (18 sts)

Row 9: Knit.

Row 10: K16, turn.

Row 11: YO, P14, turn.

Row 12: YO, K12, turn.

Row 13: YO, P10, turn.

Row 14: YO, K8, turn.

Row 15: YO, P6, turn.

Row 16: YO, K6, [K2tog, K1] 3 times.

Row 17: P12, (SSP, P1) 3 times. (18 sts)

Row 18: Purl.

Row 19: P16, turn.

Row 20: K14, turn.

Row 21: P12, turn.

Row 22: YO, K10, turn.

Row 23: YO, P8, turn.

Row 24: YO, K6, turn.

Row 25: YO, P6, SSP, P1, SSP twice, P1.

Row 26: K11, K2tog, K1, K2tog twice, K1. (16 sts)

Row 27: Knit.

Row 28: K14, turn.

Row 29: P12, turn.

Row 30: K10, turn.

Row 31: YO, P8, turn.

Row 32: YO, K6, turn.

Row 33: YO, P4, turn.

Row 34: YO, K4, K2tog, K1, K2tog twice, K1.

Row 35: P9, SSP, P1, SSP twice, P1. (14 sts)

Row 36: Purl.

Row 37: P12, turn.

Row 38: K10, turn.

Row 39: P8, turn.

Row 40: YO, K6, turn.

Row 41: YO, P6, SSP twice, P1.

Row 42: K9, K2tog twice, K1. (12 sts)

Row 43: Knit.

Row 44: K10, turn.

Row 45: P8, turn.

Row 46: K6, turn.

Row 47: YO, P4, turn.

Row 48: YO, K4, K2tog twice, K1.

Row 49: P7, SSP twice, P1. (10 sts)

Row 50: Purl.

Row 51: P8, turn.

Row 52: K6, turn.

Row 53: P4, turn.

Row 54: YO, K2, turn.

Row 55: YO, P2, SSP twice, P1.

Row 56: K5, K2tog twice, K1. (8 sts)

Row 57–58: Knit 2 rows.

Row 59: Purl.

Row 60: K2, K2tog, SSK, K2. (6 sts)

Row 61: Purl.

Row 62: K1, K2tog, SSK, K1. (4 sts)

Row 63: Purl.

Cut yarn leaving a long tail. Using a tapestry needle, thread tail through the stitches left on needle and pull up tight to gather stitches.

BODY

Using 2.75mm straight needles and Yarn B, cast on 8 sts.

Rows 1–15: As Rows 1–15 of Standard Body – Plain.

Row 16: [K16, M1] 3 times, K to end. (60 sts)

Row 17: P18, K10, P4, K10, P to end. (The knit stitches on this row mark the leg positions.)

Row 18: [K1, MB] 9 times, K10, [K1, MB] twice, K10, [K1, MB] 8 times, K2.

Row 19: Purl.

Row 20: K2, [MB, K1] to end.

Row 21: Purl.

Row 22: [K1, MB] to last 2 sts, K2.

Rows 23–34: Rpt last 4 rows 3 more times.

Row 35: P1, SSP, P14, SSP twice, P18, SSP twice, P14, SSP, P1. (54 sts)

Row 36: [K1, MB] to last 2 sts, K2.

Rows 37–40: Rpt Rows 19–22.

Rows 41–42: Rpt Rows 19–20.

Row 43: P1, P2tog, P12, P2tog twice, P16, P2tog twice, P12, P2tog, P1. (48 sts)

Rows 44–46: Rpt Rows 20–22.

Rows 47–48: Rpt Rows 19–20.

Row 49: P1, P2tog, P10, P2tog twice, P14, P2tog twice, P10, P2tog, P1. (42 sts)

Rows 50–52: Rpt Rows 20–22.

Rows 53–54: Rpt Rows 19–20.

Row 55: P1, P2tog, P8, P2tog twice, P12, P2tog twice, P8, P2tog, P1. (36 sts)

Rows 56–58: Rpt Rows 20–22.

Row 59: P1, SSP, P6, SSP twice, P10, SSP twice, P6, SSP, P1. (30 sts)

Row 60: As Row 22.

Rows 61–62: Rpt Rows 19–20.

Row 63: P1, P2tog, P4, P2tog twice, P8, P2tog twice, P4, P2tog, P1. (24 sts)

Rows 64–65: Rpt Rows 20–21.

Row 66: K1, [K1, K2tog] to last 2 sts, K2. (17 sts)

Row 67: Purl.

Row 68: K2tog to last st, K1. (9 sts)

Row 69: Purl.

Cut yarn leaving a long tail. Using a tapestry needle, thread tail through the stitches left on needle and pull up tight to gather stitches.

ARMS (MAKE 2)

Work as Standard Arms (see Standard Body Parts).

LEGS (MAKE 2)

Work as Standard Legs – Plain (see Standard Body Parts).

MAKING UP

Follow the instructions in the techniques section (see Techniques: Making Up Your Animal).

OUTFIT PATTERNS

SAILOR SWEATER

The sweater is worked top down, with raglan sleeves and no seams. The top half is worked back and forth in rows, and the body and sleeves are worked in the round.

Using 3.5mm straight needles and Yarn A, cast on 36 sts.

Row 1 (ws): Purl.

Rows 2–4: Stocking stitch 3 rows.

Row 5: Cast on 3 sts using the Purl cast-on method (see Techniques: Casting On and Stitches), P9, pm, P12, pm, P6, pm, purl to end. (39 sts)

Row 6: P3, K1, m1l, [knit to marker, m1r, sm, K1, m1l] 3 times, knit to last 4 sts, m1r, K1, P3. (47 sts)

Row 7 (buttonhole row): Purl to last 2 sts, YO, P2tog.

Row 8: P3, K1, m1l, [knit to marker, m1r, sm, K1, m1l] 3 times, knit to last 4 sts, m1r, K1, P3. (55 sts)

Row 9: Purl.

Rows 10–12: Rpt last 2 rows once more, then rpt Row 8 again. (71 sts)

Row 13 (buttonhole row): Purl to last 2 sts, YO, P2tog.

Rows 14–18: Rpt Rows 8-12. (95 sts)

Change to Yarn B.

Row 19 (buttonhole row): Purl to last 2 sts, YO, P2tog.

Row 20: P3, K1, m1l, [knit to marker, m1r, sm, K1, m1l] 3 times, knit to last 4 sts, m1r, K1, P3. (103 sts)

Change to Yarn A.

Row 21: Purl.

Row 22: P3, K1, m1l, [knit to marker, m1r, sm, K1, m1l] 3 times, knit to last 4 sts, m1r, K1, P3. (111 sts)

Change to Yarn B.

Row 23: Purl.

Row 24: Transfer sts to a 3.5mm circular needle, P3, K1, m1l, [knit to marker, m1r, sm, K1, m1l] 3 times, knit to last 4 sts, m1r, K1, slip the last 3 sts (without working them) onto a cable needle. (119 sts)

Join to work in the round:

Rnd 25: Position cable needle behind first 3 sts on LH needle, place marker for beginning of round, knit first st on LH needle together with first st on cable needle, rpt for next 2 sts, *K1, [K1, P2] to 1 stitch before marker, K1, sm, K1 (back), without working them place next 25 sts onto waste yarn (sleeve)*, remove marker; rpt from * to * (front and sleeve). (66 sts)

Rnd 26: K1, m1l, knit to marker, m1r, sm, K2, m1l, knit to last st, m1r, K1. (70 sts)

Rnds 27–28: Knit 2 rnds.

Rnd 29: K3, [P2, K1] to 1 st before marker, K1, sm, K4, [P2, K1] to last 2 sts, K2.

Rnds 30–32: Rpt Rnds 26-28. (74 sts)

Rnd 33: [K1, P2] to marker, sm, K1, [K1, P2] to last st, K1.

Rnds 34–36: Rpt Rnds 26-28. (78 sts)

Rnd 37: K1, [K1, P2] to 1 st before marker, K1, sm, K2, [K1, P2] to last 2 sts, K2.

Rnds 38–40: Rpt Rnds 26-28. (82 sts)

Rnd 41: K2, [K1, P2] to 2 sts before marker, K2, sm, K3, [K1, P2] to last 3 sts, K3.

Rnds 42–44: Knit 3 rnds.

Rnd 45: K2, [K1, P2] to 2 sts before marker, K2, sm, K3, [K1, P2] to last 3 sts, K3.

Rnd 46: Knit.

Change to 3mm circular needle.

Rnd 47: Knit.

Rnd 48: Purl.

Cast off.

SLEEVES

Starting at under arm, slip the 25 sts held on waste yarn for one sleeve evenly onto three 3.5mm dpns and rejoin Yarn B.

Using fourth dpn, start knitting in the round.

Rnd 1: [K1, P2] to last st, K1.

Rnds 2–3: Knit 2 rnds.

Rnd 4: K1, m1l, knit to last st, m1r, K1. (27 sts)

Rnd 5: K1, [K1, P2] to last 2 sts, K2.

Rnds 6–8: Knit 3 rnds.

Rnd 9: K1, [K1, P2] to last 2 sts, K2.

Rnds 10–11: Knit 2 rnds.

Rnd 12: K1, m1l, knit to last st, m1r, K1. (29 sts)

Rnd 13: K2, [K1, P2] to last 3 sts, K3.

Rnds 14–16: Knit 3 rnds.

Rnds 17–22: Rpt Rnds 13-16 once more, then rpt Rnds 13-14 again.

Change to a set of 3mm dpns.

Rnd 23: Knit.

Rnd 24: Purl.

Cast off.

Repeat for second sleeve.

MAKING UP

1. If necessary, close hole under arm with a couple of stitches.

2. Block the sweater.

3. Sew buttons in place on left-hand button band, matching them up with the buttonholes.

CARGO SHORTS

The shorts are worked top down with no seams, except for the pockets which are made separately and sewn on afterwards. The top part is worked back and forth with a button band down the back and some short row shaping for the bottom; the lower half and legs are worked in the round.

Using 3mm straight needles and Yarn C, cast on 52 sts.

Row 1 (ws): Knit.

Row 2: Knit.

Row 3 (buttonhole row): Knit to last 3 sts, K2tog, YO, K1.

Rows 4–5: Knit 2 rows.

Change to 3.5mm straight needles.

Row 6: [K1, K1fb] 11 times, K1fb 3 times, K1, K1fb 4 times, [K1, K1fb] 10 times, K2. (80 sts)

Row 7: K2, P8, turn.

Row 8: YO, knit to end.

Row 9: K2, P8, SSP, P2, turn.

Row 10: YO, knit to end.

Row 11: K2, P11, SSP, P2, turn.

Row 12: YO, knit to end.

Row 13: K2, P14, SSP, P2, turn.

Row 14: YO, knit to end.

Row 15: K2, P17, SSP, purl to last 2 sts, K2.

Row 16: K10, turn.

Row 17: YO, purl to last 2 sts, K2.

Row 18: K10, K2tog, K2, turn.

Row 19 (buttonhole row): YO, purl to last 3 sts, P2tog, YO, K1.

Row 20: K13, K2tog, K2, turn.

Row 21: YO, purl to last 2 sts, K2.

Row 22: K16, K2tog, K2, turn.

Row 23: YO, purl to last 2 sts, K2.

Row 24: K19, K2tog, knit to end.

Row 25: K2, purl to last 2 sts, K2.

Row 26: Knit.

Row 27 (buttonhole row): K2, purl to last 3 sts, P2tog, YO, K1.

Row 28: Knit.

Row 29: K2, purl to last 2 sts, K2.

Rows 30–31: Rpt last 2 rows once more.

Row 32: Transfer sts to a 3.5mm circular needle and knit to last 2 sts, slip the last 2 sts (without working them) onto a cable needle.

Join to work in the round:

Rnd 33: Position the cable needle behind the first 2 sts on the LH needle, knit first st on LH needle together with first st on cable needle, place marker for beginning of round, knit next st on LH needle together with remaining st on cable needle, knit to end. (78 sts)

Rnds 34–37: Knit 4 rnds.

Rnd 38: K1, m1l, knit to last st, m1r, K1. (80 sts)

Rnds 39–40: Knit 2 rnds.

Rnd 41: K1, m1l, knit to last st, m1r, K1. (82 sts)

Rnd 42: K40, m1r, K2, m1l, knit to end. (84 sts)

Rnd 43: K1, m1l, knit to last st, m1r, K1. (86 sts)

Rnd 44: Knit.

Rnd 45: K1, m1l, K41, m1r, K2, m1l, K41, m1r, K1. (90 sts)

Rnd 46: Knit.

Rnd 47: K1, m1l, K43, m1r, K2, m1l, K43, m1r, K1. (94 sts)

Rnd 48: Knit.

Divide for legs:

Rnd 49: K47 (right leg), without working them place next 47 sts onto waste yarn (left leg).

RIGHT LEG

Rnds 50–53: Knit 4 rnds.

Rnd 54: SSK, K22, K2tog, knit to end. (45 sts)

Rnds 55–59: Knit 5 rnds.

Rnd 60: SSK, K20, K2tog, knit to end. (43 sts)

Rnds 61–65: Knit 5 rnds.

Rnd 66: SSK, K18, K2tog, knit to end. (41 sts)

Rnds 67–69: Knit 3 rnds.

Change to 3mm circular needle.

Rnd 70: Knit.

Rnd 71: Purl.

Rnds 72–73: Rpt last 2 rnds once more.

Cast off.

LEFT LEG

Rnd 49: Transfer sts from waste yarn to 3.5mm circular needle, rejoin yarn and knit 1 rnd placing marker for beginning of rnd. (47 sts)

Rnds 50–53: Knit 4 rnds.

Rnd 54: K21, SSK, K22, K2tog. (45 sts)

Rnds 55–59: Knit 5 rnds.

Rnd 60: K21, SSK, K20, K2tog. (43 sts)

Rnds 61–65: Knit 5 rnds.

Rnd 66: K21, SSK, K18, K2tog. (41 sts)

Rnds 67–69: Knit 3 rnds.

Change to 3mm circular needle.

Rnd 70: Knit.

Rnd 71: Purl.

Rnds 72–73: Rpt last 2 rnds once more.

Cast off.

POCKET (MAKE 2)

Using Yarn C and 3mm straight needles, cast on 17 sts.

Row 1 (ws): Knit.

Change to 3.5mm straight needles.

Row 2 (buttonhole row): K8, YO, K2tog, knit to end.

Rows 3–16: Stocking stitch 14 rows.

Row 17: P4, P2tog, P5, SSP, P4. (15 sts)

Cast off.

MAKING UP

1. If necessary, close hole where the 2 legs join with a couple of stitches.

2. Block shorts and pockets.

3. Position pockets on the side of each leg, central to the line of decreases and about 2cm (¾in) up from the hem. Pin in place. Sew around 3 sides leaving top of pocket open.

4. Sew buttons in place on left-hand button band down back of pants and at the top of the pockets, matching them up with the buttonholes.

T-BAR SHOES

Using 2.75mm needles and Yarn D for the soles, follow the pattern for the T-Bar Shoes (see Shoes and Accessories), changing to Yarn C for the upper parts of the shoes.

EWE

If you would rather make a ewe than a ram that's easy to achieve. Just omit the ram's horns and sew the ears on slightly further back than you would for the ram, as shown in this photograph.

LOUIS
THE OWL

Little Louis is very excited about his trip to the lifeboat
station! In his cable knit sweater and joggers, and
bright yellow duffle coa,t he's ready for the most
ferocious weather. He'd like to be a lifeboat captain
when he's bigger, or maybe a lighthouse keeper.

YOU WILL NEED

FOR LOUIS' BODY

• Scheepjes Stonewashed
(50g/130m; 78% cotton/22%
acrylic) yarn in the
following shades:

   - *Yarn A* Grey *(Smokey Quartz
   802), 2 balls*

   - *Yarn B* Cream *(Moonstone
   801), 1 ball*

   - *Yarn C* Mustard *(Yellow Jasper
   809), 1 ball*

• 2.75mm (US 2) straight needles

• Toy stuffing

• 2 x 10mm (½in) buttons

FOR LOUIS' OUTFIT

• Scheepjes Catona (10g/25m,
25g/62m or 50g/125m;
100% cotton) yarn in the
following shades:

   - *Yarn A* Cream *(Old Lace 130),
   1 x 50g ball and 1 x 10g ball*

   - *Yarn B* Mustard *(Saffron 249),
   1 x 50g ball and 1 x 10g ball*

   - *Yarn C* Grey Blue *(Charcoal
   393), 1 x 50g ball*

• 2.75mm (US 2) straight needles

• 3mm (US 2½) straight needles

• 3mm (US 2½) circular
needle (23cm/9in length)

• Set of four 3mm (US 2½)
double-pointed needles

• 3.5mm (US 4) straight needles

• 3.5mm (US 4) circular
needle (23cm/9in length)

• Set of four 3.5mm (US 4)
double-pointed needles

• Waste yarn

• Cable needle

• 6 small buttons

• 3 small wooden toggles
(approx 20mm/¾in long)

OWL PATTERN

HEAD

Starting at neck:

Using 2.75mm straight needles and Yarn A, cast on 11 sts.

Row 1 (ws): Purl.

Row 2: [K1, M1] to last st, K1. (21 sts)

Row 3: Purl.

Row 4: [K2, M1] to last st, K1. (31 sts)

Row 5: Purl.

Row 6: K1, m1l, K6, m1r, K1, m1l, K7, sl1, K7, m1r, K1, m1l, K6, m1r, K1. (37 sts)

Row 7: Purl.

Row 8: K1, m1l, K8, m1r, K1, m1l, K8, sl1, K8, m1r, K1, m1l, K8, m1r, K1. (43 sts)

Row 9: Purl.

Row 10: K1, m1l, K10, m1r, K1, m1l, K9, sl1, K9, m1r, K1, m1l, K10, m1r, K1. (49 sts)

Row 11: Purl.

Row 12: K1, m1l, K12, m1r, K1, m1l, K10, sl1, K10, m1r, K1, m1l, K12, m1r, K1. (55 sts)

Row 13: Purl.

Row 14: (A) K21, (B) K6, sl1, K6, (A) K21.

Row 15: (A) P19, (B) P17, (A) P19.

Row 16: (A) K1, m1l, K14, m1r, K1, m1l, K2, (B) K19, (A) K2, m1r, K1, m1l, K14, m1r, K1. (61 sts)

Row 17: (A) P21, (B) P19, (A) P21.

Row 18: (A) K20, (B) K21, (A) K20.

Row 19: (A) P20, (B) P21, (A) P20.

Row 20: (A) K19, (B) K23, (A) K19.

Row 21: (A) P19, (B) P23, (A) P19.

Rows 22–26: Rpt last 2 rows twice more, then rpt Row 20 again.

Row 27: (A) P20, (B) P10, (A) P1, (B) P10, (A) P20.

Row 28: (A) K1, K2tog, K13, CDD, K1, (B) K10, sl1, K10, (A) K1, CDD, K13, SSK, K1. (55 sts)

Row 29: (A) P18, (B) P8, (A) P3, (B) P8, (A) P18.

Row 30: (A) K18, (B) K8, (A) K1, sl1, K1, (B) K8, (A) K18.

Row 31: (A) P19, (B) P6, (A) P5, (B) P6, (A) P19.

Row 32: (A) K1, K2tog, K11, CDD, K3, (B) K4, (A) K3, sl1, K3, (B) K4, (A) K3, CDD, K11, SSK, K1. (49 sts)

Continue in Yarn A only.

Row 33: Purl.

Row 34: K24, sl1, K24.

Row 35: Purl.

Row 36: K1, K2tog, K9, CDD, K9, sl1, K9, CDD, K9, SSK, K1. (43 sts)

Row 37: Purl.

Row 38: K1, K2tog, K7, CDD, K8, sl1, K8, CDD, K7, SSK, K1. (37 sts)

Row 39: Purl.

Row 40: K1, K2tog, K3, K2tog 4 times, K3, CDD, K3, SSK 4 times, K3, SSK, K1. (25 sts)

Row 41: Purl.

Row 42: K1, K2tog 5 times, CDD, SSK 5 times, K1. (13 sts)

Row 43: Purl.

Cast off.

BEAK

Using 2.75mm straight needles and Yarn C, cast on 11 sts.

Row 1 (ws): P7, turn.

Row 2: YO, K3, turn.

Row 3: YO, P3, SSP, P1, turn.

Row 4: YO, K5, K2tog, K1, turn.

Row 5: YO, P7, SSP, P1.

Row 6: K4, CDD, K2, K2tog, K1. (9 sts)

Row 7: Purl.

Row 8: K3, CDD, K3. (7 sts)

Row 9: P2, PCDD, P2. (5 sts)

Cut yarn leaving a long tail. Using a tapestry needle, thread tail through the stitches left on needle and pull up tight to gather stitches.

EARS (MAKE 2)

Using 2.75mm straight needles and Yarn A, cast on 17 sts.

Row 1 (ws): Purl.

Row 2: [K3, K2tog, SSK] twice, K3. (13 sts)

Row 3: Purl.

Row 4: K1, [K1, K2tog, SSK] twice, K2. (9 sts)

Row 5: Purl.

Row 6: K1, K2tog, sl1 kw, K2tog, PSSO, SSK, K1. (5 sts)

Row 7: Purl.

Row 8: Knit.

Cut yarn leaving a long tail. Using a tapestry needle, thread tail through the stitches left on needle and pull up tight to gather stitches.

BODY

Work as Standard Body – Contrast Front (see Standard Body Parts).

ARMS (MAKE 2)

Work as Standard Arms (see Standard Body Parts).

LEGS (MAKE 2)

Work as Standard Leg – Plain (see Standard Body Parts).

MAKING UP

Follow the instructions in the techniques section (see Techniques: Making Up Your Animal).

OUTFIT PATTERNS

CABLE SWEATER

The sweater is worked top down, with raglan sleeves and no seams. The top half is worked back and forth in rows with a button band opening at the back, and the body and sleeves are worked in the round.

Using 3mm straight needles and Yarn A, cast on 49 sts.

Row 1 (ws): [K1, P1] to last st, K1.

Row 2: [P1, K1] to last st, P1.

Rows 3–9: Rpt last 2 rows 3 more times, then rpt Row 1 again.

Change to 3.5mm straight needles.

The even numbered rows now become the wrong side of the work so that the right sides of the rolled collar are facing when folded over.

Row 10 (ws): K3, P5, pm, K2, P3, K2, P1, pm, [K2, P3] 3 times, K2, P1, pm, K2, P3, K2, P1, pm, purl to last 3 sts, K3.

Row 11 (buttonhole row): K1, YO, K2tog, knit to marker, m1r, sm, K1, m1l, P2, K3, P2, m1r, sm, K1, m1l, [P2, K3] 3 times, P2, m1r, sm, K1, m1l, P2, K3, P2, m1r, sm, K1, m1l, knit to end. (57 sts)

Row 12: K3, P7, [K2, P3] 7 times, K2, purl to last 3 sts, K3.

Row 13: *Knit to marker, m1r, sm, K1, m1l, K1, place pattern marker, P2, K3, P2*; rpt from * to * once more, [K3, P2] twice; rpt from * to * once, knit to marker, m1r, sm, K1, m1l, knit to end. (65 sts)

Row 14: K3, P9, K2, P1fb, P2, K2, P5, [K2, P1fb, P2] 3 times, K2, P5, K2, P1fb, P2, K2, purl to last 3 sts, K3. (70 sts)

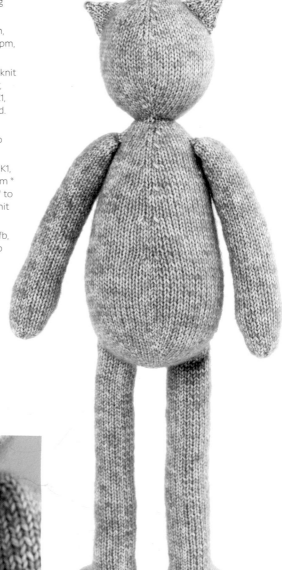

Row 15: *Knit to marker, m1r, sm, K1, m1l, knit to pattern marker, P2, C4F, P2*; rpt from * to * once more, [C4F, P2] twice; rpt from * to * once, knit to marker, m1r, sm, K1, m1l, knit to end. (78 sts)

Row 16: K3, P11, K2, P4, K2, P7, [K2, P4] 3 times, K2, P7, K2, P4, K2, purl to last 3 sts, K3.

Row 17 (buttonhole row): K1, YO, K2tog, *knit to marker, m1r, sm, K1, m1l, knit to pattern marker, P2, K4, P2*; rpt from * to * once more, [K4, P2] twice; rpt from * to * once, knit to marker, m1r, sm, K1, m1l, knit to end. (86 sts)

Row 18: K3, P13, K2, P4, K2, P9, [K2, P4] 3 times, K2, P9, K2, P4, K2, purl to last 3 sts, K3.

Row 19: *Knit to marker, m1r, sm, K1, m1l, knit to pattern marker, P2, K4, P2*; rpt from * to * once more, [K4, P2] twice; rpt from * to * once, knit to marker, m1r, sm, K1, m1l, knit to end. (94 sts)

Row 20: K3, P15, K2, P4, K2, P11, [K2, P4] 3 times, K2, P11, K2, P4, K2, purl to last 3 sts, K3.

Row 21: As Row 15. (102 sts)

Row 22: K3, P17, K2, P4, K2, P13, [K2, P4] 3 times, K2, P13, K2, P4, K2, purl to last 3 sts, K3.

Row 23 (buttonhole row): As Row 17. (110 sts)

Row 24: K3, P19, K2, P4, K2, P15, [K2, P4] 3 times, K2, P15, K2, P4, K2, purl to last 3 sts, K3.

Row 25: As Row 19. (118 sts)

Row 26: K3, P21, K2, P4, K2, P17, [K2, P4] 3 times, K2, P17, K2, P4, K2, purl to last 3 sts, K3.

Row 27: As Row 15. (126 sts)

Row 28: K3, P23, K2, P4, K2, P19, [K2, P4] 3 times, K2, P19, K2, P4, K2, purl to last 3 sts, K3.

Row 29: Transfer sts to a 3.5mm circular needle, *knit to marker, m1r, sm, K1, m1l, knit to pattern marker, P2, K4, P2*; rpt from * to * once more, [K4, P2] twice; rpt from * to * once, knit to marker, m1r, sm, K1, m1l, knit to last 3 sts, slip the last 3 sts (without working them) onto a cable needle. (134 sts)

Join to work in the round:

Rnd 30: Position cable needle behind first 3 sts on LH needle, place marker for beginning of round, knit first st on LH needle together with first st on cable needle; rpt for next 2 sts, knit to marker, sm, K1 (right back), without working them place next 28 sts and pattern marker onto waste yarn (sleeve), remove marker, knit to pattern marker, [P2, K4] 3 times, P2, knit to marker, sm K1 (front), without working them place next 28 sts and pattern marker onto waste yarn (sleeve), remove marker, knit to end (left back). (75 sts)

Rnd 31: *Knit to marker, m1r, sm, K2, m1l, knit to pattern marker, [P2, K4] 3 times, P2, knit to marker, m1r, sm, K2, m1l, knit to end. (79 sts)

Rnd 32: Knit to pattern marker, [P2, K4] 3 times, P2, knit to end.

Rnd 33: Knit to pattern marker, [P2, C4F] 3 times, P2, knit to end.

Rnd 34: As Rnd 32.

Rnd 35: As Rnd 31. (83 sts)

Rnds 36–38: Rpt Rnd 32 3 times.

Rnd 39: *Knit to marker, m1r, sm, K2, m1l, knit to pattern marker, [P2, C4F] 3 times, P2, knit to marker, m1r, sm, K2, m1l, knit to end. (87 sts)

Rnds 40–42: Rpt Rnd 32 3 times.

Rnds 43–45: Rpt Rnds 31-33. (91 sts)

Rnd 46: As Rnd 32.

Rnd 47: Knit to pattern marker, [P2, K1, K2tog, K1] 3 times, P2, knit to end. (88 sts)

Rnd 48: Knit to pattern marker, [P2, K3] 3 times, P2, knit to end.

Change to 3mm circular needle.

Rnd 49: [K1, P1] to 1 stitch before pattern marker, K1, [P2tog, K1, P1, K1] 3 times, P2tog, [K1, P1] to end. (84 sts)

Rnd 50: [K1, P1] to end.

Rnds 51–53: Rpt Rnd 50 3 more times.

Cast off in pattern.

SLEEVES

Starting at under arm, slip the 28 sts held on waste yarn for one sleeve evenly onto three 3.5mm dpns and rejoin yarn.

Using fourth dpn, start knitting in the round.

Rnd 1: Knit to pattern marker, P2, K4, P2, knit to end.

Rnds 2–3: Rpt Rnd 1 twice more.

Rnd 4: K1, m1l, knit to pattern marker, P2, C4F, P2, knit to last st, m1r, K1. (30 sts)

Rnds 5–9: Rpt Rnd 1, 5 times.

Rnd 10: Knit to pattern marker, P2, C4F, P2, knit to end.

Rnd 11: As Rnd 1.

Rnd 12: K1, m1l, knit to pattern marker, P2, K4, P2, knit to last st, m1r, K1. (32 sts)

Rnds 13-15: Rpt Rnd 1, 3 times.

Rnd 16: As Rnd 10.

Rnd 17: As Rnd 1.

Rnd 18: Knit to pattern marker, P2, K1, K2tog, K1, P2, knit to end. (31 sts)

Rnd 19: Knit to pattern marker, P2, K3, P2, knit to end.

Change to a set of 3mm dpns.

Rnd 20: [P1, K1] to pattern marker, P2tog, K1, P1, K1, P2tog, [K1, P1] to end. (29 sts)

Rnd 21: [P1, K1] to last st, P1.

Rnds 22–24: Rpt Rnd 21 3 more times.

Cast off in pattern.

Repeat for second sleeve.

MAKING UP

1. If necessary, close hole under arm with a couple of stitches.

2. Block sweater.

3. Sew buttons in place on left-hand button band, matching them up with the buttonholes.

4. Double over neck band.

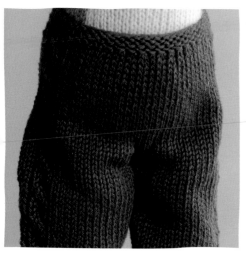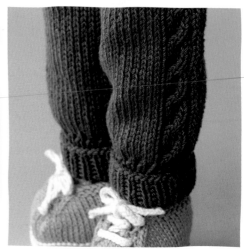

CABLE JOGGERS

The joggers are worked top down and seamlessly. The top part is worked back and forth with a button band down the back and some short row shaping for the bottom; the lower half and legs are worked in the round.

Using 3mm straight needles and Yarn C, cast on 52 sts.

Row 1 (ws): Knit.

Row 2: Knit.

Row 3 (buttonhole row): Knit to last 3 sts, K2tog, YO, K1.

Rows 4–5: Knit 2 rows.

Change to 3.5mm straight needles.

Row 6: [K1, K1fb] 11 times, K1fb 3 times, K1, K1fb 4 times, [K1, K1fb] 10 times, K2. (80 sts)

Row 7: K2, P7, turn.

Row 8: YO, knit to end.

Row 9: K2, P7, SSP, P2, turn.

Row 10: YO, knit to end.

Row 11: K2, P10, SSP, P2, turn.

Row 12: YO, knit to end.

Row 13: K2, P13, SSP, P2, turn.

Row 14: YO, knit to end.

Row 15: K2, P16, SSP, K1, P4, K1, P30, K1, P4, K1, purl to last 2 sts, K2.

Row 16: K9, turn.

Row 17: YO, purl to last 2 sts, K2.

Row 18: K9, K2tog, K2, turn.

Row 19 (buttonhole row): YO, purl to last 3 sts, P2tog, YO, K1.

Row 20: K12, K2tog, K2, turn.

Row 21: YO, purl to last 2 sts, K2.

Row 22: K15, K2tog, K2, turn.

Row 23: YO, purl to last 2 sts, K2.

Row 24: K18, K2tog, P1, K4, P1, K30, P1, K4, P1, knit to end.

Row 25: K2, P17, K1, P4, K1, place pattern marker, P30, K1, P4, K1, place pattern marker, purl to last 2 sts, K2.

Row 26: [Knit to pattern marker, P1, C4F, P1] twice, knit to end.

Row 27 (buttonhole row): K2, [purl to 6 sts before pattern marker, K1, P4, K1] twice, purl to last 3 sts, P2tog, YO, K1.

Row 28: [Knit to pattern marker, P1, K4, P1] twice, knit to end.

Row 29: K2, [purl to 6 sts before pattern marker, K1, P4, K1] 2 times, purl to last 2 sts, K2.

Rows 30–31: Rpt last 2 rows once more.

Row 32: Transfer sts to a 3.5mm circular needle, [knit to pattern marker, P1, C4F, P1] twice, knit to last 2 sts, slip the last 2 sts (without working them) onto a cable needle.

Join to work in the round:

Rnd 33: Position the cable needle behind the first 2 sts on the LH needle, knit first st on LH needle together with first st on cable needle, place marker for beginning of round, knit next st on LH needle together with remaining st on cable needle, [knit to pattern marker, P1, K4, P1] twice, knit to end. (78 sts)

Rnd 34: [Knit to pattern marker, P1, K4, P1] twice, knit to end.

Rnds 35–37: Rpt Rnd 34 3 more times.

Rnd 38: K1, m1l, [knit to pattern marker, P1, C4F, P1] twice, knit to last st, m1r, K1. (80 sts)

Rnds 39–40: Rpt Rnd 34 twice.

Rnd 41: K1, m1l, [knit to pattern marker, P1, K4, P1] twice, knit to last st, m1r, K1. (82 sts)

Rnd 42: Knit to pattern marker, P1, K4, P1, K14, m1r, K2, m1l, knit to pattern marker, P1, K4, P1, knit to end. (84 sts)

Rnd 43: As Rnd 41. (86 sts)

Rnd 44: [Knit to pattern marker, P1, C4F, P1] twice, knit to end.

Rnd 45: K1, m1l, knit to pattern marker, P1, K4, P1, K15, m1r, K2, m1l, knit to pattern marker, P1, K4, P1, knit to last st, m1r, K1. (90 sts)

Rnd 46: As Rnd 34.

Rnd 47: K1, m1l, knit to pattern marker, P1, K4, P1, K16, m1r, K2, m1l, knit to pattern marker, P1, K4, P1, knit to last st, m1r, K1. (94 sts)

Rnd 48: Rpt Rnd 34.

Divide for legs:

Rnd 49: Knit to pattern marker, P1, K4, P1, K18 (right leg), without working them place next 47 sts and pattern marker onto waste yarn (left leg).

RIGHT LEG

Rnd 50: Knit to pattern marker, P1, C4F, P1, knit to end.

Rnd 51: Knit to pattern marker, P1, K4, P1, knit to end.

Rnds 52–53: Rpt Rnd 51 twice more.

Rnd 54: SSK, knit to 2 sts before pattern marker, K2tog, P1, K4, P1, knit to end. (45 sts)

Rnd 55: As Rnd 51.

Rnd 56: As Rnd 50.

Rnds 57–61: Rpt Rnd 51 5 times.

Rnds 62–85: Rpt Rnds 50–61 twice more. (41 sts)

Rnds 86–91: Rpt Rnds 56–61.

Rnds 92–93: Rpt Rnds 50–51.

Rnd 94: Knit to pattern marker, P1, K1, K2tog, K1, P1, knit to end. (40 sts)

Change to a set of 3mm dpns.

Rnd 95: [K1, P1] to end.

Rnds 96–110: Rpt last rnd 15 more times.

Cast off in pattern.

LEFT LEG

Rnd 49: Transfer sts from waste yarn to 3.5mm circular needle, rejoin yarn and placing a marker for beginning of rnd, knit to pattern marker, P1, K4, P1, knit to end.

Rnd 50: Knit to pattern marker, P1, C4F, P1, knit to end.

Rnd 51: Knit to pattern marker, P1, K4, P1, knit to end.

Rnds 52–53: Rpt Rnd 51 twice more.

Rnd 54: Knit to pattern marker, P1, K4, P1, SSK, knit to last 2 sts, K2tog. (45 sts)

Rnd 55: As Rnd 51.

Rnd 56: As Rnd 50.

Rnds 57–61: Rpt Rnd 51 5 times.

Rnds 62–85: Rpt Rnds 50–61 twice more. (41 sts)

Rnds 86–91: Rpt Rnds 56–61.

Rnds 92–93: Rpt Rnds 50–51.

Rnd 94: Knit to pattern marker, P1, K1, K2tog, K1, P1, knit to end. (40 sts)

Change to a set of 3mm dpns.

Rnd 95: [P1, K1] to end.

Rnds 96–110: Rpt last rnd 15 more times.

Cast off in pattern.

MAKING UP

1. If necessary, close hole where the 2 legs join with a couple of stitches.

2. Block joggers.

3. Sew buttons in place on left-hand button band down back of joggers, matching them up with the buttonholes.

4. Turn up cuffs.

DUFFLE COAT

The coat is worked top down, seamlessly, with raglan sleeves and a vent at the back. The coat is worked back and forth in rows and the sleeves are worked in the round.

Using 3mm straight needles and Yarn B, cast on 45 sts.

Row 1 (ws): Knit.

Row 2: K8, pm, K7, pm, K14, pm, K7, pm, knit to end.

Change to 3.5mm straight needles.

Row 3: K6, purl to last 6 sts, K6.

Row 4: [Knit to marker, m1r, sm, K1, m1l] 4 times, knit to end. (53 sts)

Row 5: As Row 3.

Row 6: As Row 4. (61 sts)

Row 7: Knit.

Row 8: As Row 4. (69 sts)

Rows 9–20: Rpt Rows 3–8 twice more. (117 sts)

Rows 21–22: Rpt Rows 3–4. (125 sts)

Row 23: K6, *purl to marker (right front), remove marker, without working them place next 26 sts onto waste yarn (sleeve), P1, sm; rpt from *, once more (back and second sleeve), purl to last 6 sts, K6 (left front). (73 sts)

Row 24: [Knit to marker, m1r, sm, K2, m1l] twice, knit to end. (77 sts)

Rows 25–26: Knit 2 rows.

Row 27: K6, purl to last 6 sts, K6.

Row 28: As Row 24. (81 sts)

Row 29: As Row 27.

Rows 30–31: Knit 2 rows.

The left and right sides of the coat are now worked separately, creating an overlapping vent down the centre back.

LEFT SIDE

Row 32: K42, without working them place next 39 sts onto a stitch holder. (42 sts)

Row 33: K2, purl to last 6 sts, K6.

Row 34: Knit to marker, m1r, sm, K2, m1l, knit to end. (44 sts)

Row 35: As Row 33.

Rows 36–38: Knit 3 rows.

Row 39: As Row 33.

Row 40: As Row 34. (46 sts)

Row 41: As Row 33.

Rows 42–49: Knit 8 rows.

Change to 3mm straight needles.

Rows 50–51: Knit 2 rows.

Cast off.

RIGHT SIDE

Row 32: Transfer the stitches on hold back onto needle. With RS facing you and starting at the centre back, pick up 3 sts from behind the first row of left side (see Techniques: Casting On and Stitches, Picking up stitches), knit to end. (42 sts)

Row 33: K6, purl to last 2 sts, K2.

Row 34: Knit to marker, m1r, sm, K2, m1l, knit to end. (44 sts)

Row 35: As Row 33.

Rows 36–38: Knit 3 rows.

Row 39: As Row 33.

Row 40: As Row 34. (46 sts)

Row 41: As Row 33.

Rows 42–49: Knit 8 rows.

Change to 3mm straight needles.

Rows 50–51: Knit 2 rows.

Cast off.

SLEEVES

Starting at under arm, slip the 26 sts held on waste yarn for one sleeve evenly onto three 3.5mm dpns and rejoin yarn.

Using fourth dpn, start knitting in the round.

Rnds 1–2: Knit 2 rnds.

Rnd 3: Purl.

Rnd 4: Knit.

Rnd 5: K1, m1l, knit to last st, m1r, K1. (28 sts)

Rnds 6–8: Knit 3 rnds.

Rnd 9: Purl.

Rnds 10–11: Knit 2 rnds.

Rnd 12: As Rnd 5. (30 sts)

Rnds 13–14: Knit 2 rnds.

Rnd 15: Purl.

Rnds 16–20: Knit 5 rnds.

Rnd 21: Purl.

Rnd 22: Knit.

Rnds 23–25: Rpt Rnds 21-22 once more, then rpt Rnd 21 again.

Change to a set of 3mm dpns.

Rnd 26: Knit.

Rnd 27: Purl.

Cast off.

Repeat for second sleeve.

HOOD

Using 3.5mm needles, with RS of coat facing and beginning and ending 3 sts from centre front edges, pick up and knit 39 sts around neck edge (see Techniques: Casting On and Stitches, Picking up stitches).

Row 1 (ws): Knit.

Rows 2–39: Knit 38 rows.

Row 40: K19, K2tog, knit to end. (38 sts)

Row 41: Knit.

Row 42: K19, leave the last 19 sts unworked on the LH needle (you now have 19 sts on each needle), cut yarn leaving a long tail (about 60cm/23½in).

Thread yarn tail on to a tapestry needle and join the top of the hood:

1. Fold the hood in half so that the stitches on each needle are lined up, one needle behind the other and with wrong sides of hood touching.

2. Hold both needles together in right hand with yarn tail at the RH side.

3. Thread yarn purlwise through the first stitch on the front needle, then purlwise through the first stitch on the back needle.

4. Thread yarn knitwise through the first stitch on front needle, dropping it off the needle.

5. Thread yarn purlwise through second stitch on front needle, leaving this stitch on the needle.

6. Repeat Steps 4 and 5 for the back needle.

Repeat Steps 4–6 until all sts have been worked.

TOGGLE LOOPS (MAKE 6)

Using Yarn A and 3mm dpns, cast on 2 sts.

Make an i-cord, 18 rows long (see Techniques: Casting On and Stitches, Making i-cord).

MAKING UP

1. If necessary, close hole under arm with a couple of stitches.

2. Block the coat.

3. Thread a toggle loop through the toggle and sew in place on the front right-hand edge of coat, sewing through the coat and over the 2 ends of the toggle loop (see photo for position), rpt for the other 2 toggles.

4. Fold a toggle loop in half and sew onto the left-hand front edge of coat in the same manner and lining it up with the toggle on the right-hand side, rpt for the other 2 toggle loops.

SNEAKERS

Using 2.75mm needles and Yarn A for the soles, follow the pattern for the Sneakers (see Shoes and Accessories), changing to Yarn B for the upper parts of the shoes. Make the laces with Yarn A.

SHOES AND ACCESSORIES

Several of the outfits share the same style of shoes, and lots of the girls have the same French knickers. To avoid repetition, I've gathered them together here.

ALL SHOE SOLES

All the shoes are worked from the sole up, back and forth in rows with a seam down the centre back and sole.

The pattern for the soles is identical for all the shoes, so whichever ones you are making, start here, then move on to the specific shoe uppers.

Using the yarn specified for the soles in the outfit you are making and 2.75mm straight needles, cast on 24 sts.

Row 1 (ws): Purl.

Row 2: K1, M1, K8, [K2, M1] twice, K10, M1, K1. (28 sts)

Row 3: Purl.

Row 4: [K1, M1] twice, K8, [K1, M1] twice, K3, [K1, M1] twice, K8, [K1, M1] twice, K1. (36 sts)

Row 5: Purl.

Row 6: [K2, M1] twice, K7, [K2, M1] twice, K4, [K2, M1] twice, K7, [K2, M1] twice, K2. (44 sts)

Row 7: Purl.

Row 8: [K3, M1] twice, K6, [K3, M1] twice, K5, [K3, M1] twice, K6, [K3, M1] twice, K3. (52 sts)

Rows 9–12: Stocking stitch 4 rows.

Row 13: Purl next stitch together with corresponding stitch 4 rows below (photo 1). To do this slip next st onto RH needle (photo 2), pick up the corresponding stitch 4 rows down by inserting tip of RH needle (from top to bottom) through the 4th purl loop down from the slipped stitch (photo 3). Insert LH needle through the back loops of both sts and purl them together (photo 4); rpt to end.

T-BAR SHOES

Knit the sole, as described in All Shoe Soles, then continue as follows:

LEFT SHOE

Change to the yarn specified in the outfit you are making.

Row 14: Purl.

Rows 15–22: Stocking stitch 8 rows.

Row 23: P16, P2tog 5 times, SSP 5 times, P16. (42 sts)

Row 24: K10, YO, K2, pass the YO st over the 2 knit sts (photo 5) (this makes the beginning of the cast-off section much neater), cast off 5 sts starting with the second of the 'K2' sts (photo 6), K9 (this includes the st from the last cast off), YO, K2, pass the YO st over the 2 knit sts, cast off 4 sts starting with the second of the 'K2' sts, K12 (this includes the st from the last cast off). (33 sts)

The top right and left sides and centre tab of the shoe are now worked separately.

RIGHT SIDE

Working across the first 12 sts only.

Row 25: Knit.

Row 26: Cast on 9 sts using Purl cast-on method (see Techniques: Casting On and Stitches), K9, K2tog, knit to end. (20 sts)

Row 27 (buttonhole row): Knit to last 3 sts, K2tog, YO, K1.

Cast off.

CENTRE TAB

Working across the centre 10 sts only, with WS facing, rejoin yarn.

Row 25: K1, P2tog, P4, SSP, K1. (8 sts)

Row 26: Knit.

Row 27: K1, P2tog, P2, SSP, K1. (6 sts)

Row 28: Knit.

Row 29: K1, P4, K1.

Rows 30–40: Rpt last 2 rows 5 more times, then rpt Row 28 again.

Cast-off row: Purl next stitch together with corresponding stitch 9 rows below [slip next st onto RH needle, pick up the corresponding stitch 9 rows down by inserting tip of RH needle (from top to bottom) through the 9th purl loop down from the slipped stitch. Insert LH needle through the back loops of both sts and purl them together], purl next stitch together with corresponding stitch 9 rows below, pass first st on RH needle over the second stitch (1 stitch cast off); rpt to end.

LEFT SIDE

With WS facing, rejoin yarn to remaining 11 sts.

Rows 25–27: Knit 3 rows.

Cast off.

RIGHT SHOE

Work Rows 1–23 as Left Shoe.

Row 24: K11, YO, K2, pass the YO st over the 2 knit sts (photo 5) (this makes the beginning of the cast-off section much neater), cast off 4 sts starting with the second of the 'K2' sts (photo 6), K9 (this includes the st from the last cast off), YO, K2, pass the YO st over the 2 knit sts, cast off 5 sts starting with the second of the 'K2' sts, K11 (this includes the st from the last cast off). (33 sts)

The top right and left sides and centre tab of the shoe are now worked separately.

RIGHT SIDE

Working across the first 11 sts only.

Rows 25–27: Knit 3 rows.

Cast off.

CENTRE TAB

Work as Left Shoe centre tab.

LEFT SIDE

Slip the remaining 12 sts onto opposite needle. With RS facing, rejoin yarn to remaining 12 sts.

Row 25: Purl.

Row 26: Cast on 9 sts using Knit cast-on method (see Techniques: Casting On and Stitches), P9, SSP, purl to end. (20 sts)

Row 27 (buttonhole row): Purl to last 3 sts, P2tog, YO, P1.

Cast off purlwise.

MAKING UP

1. Sew the edges of the shoe together, working from the ankle down to the sole and to the toe.

2. Pull strap through the top of the central tab. The easiest way to do this is to thread a scrap piece of yarn through the buttonhole on the end of the strap, then thread the yarn on to a tapestry needle. Push the needle through the opening at the top of the central tab, carefully pulling the strap through (photos 7 and 8).

3. Sew button in place on opposite side of shoe to strap, lining it up with the buttonhole.

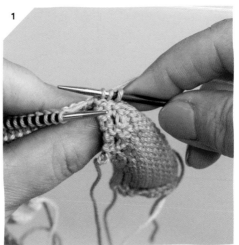
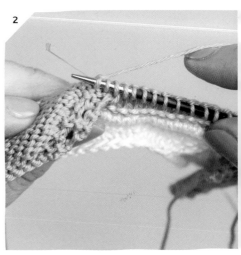

SNEAKERS (MAKE 2)

Knit the soles, as described in All Shoe Soles, then continue as follows:

LEFT SHOE

Change to the yarn specified in the outfit you are making.

Row 14: Purl.

Rows 15–17: Stocking stitch 3 rows.

The centre tongue, left and right sides of the sneakers are now worked separately.

LEFT SIDE

Row 18: K20, without working them place the remaining 32 sts onto a stitch holder. (20 sts)

Row 19: P3, m1pr, purl to end. (21 sts)

Row 20: Knit.

Row 21: K3, purl to end.

Row 22 (buttonhole row): K19, YO, K2tog.

Row 23: K3, P2tog, purl to end. (20 sts)

Row 24: K15, K2tog, K3. (19 sts)

Row 25: K3, P2tog, purl to end. (18 sts)

Row 26 (buttonhole row): K13, K2tog, K1, YO, K2tog. (17 sts)

Row 27: K3, K2tog, knit to end. (16 sts)

Row 28: K11, K2tog, K3. (15 sts)

Row 29 (buttonhole row): K2tog, K1, YO, K2tog, knit to end. (14 sts)

Cast off.

RIGHT SIDE

Transfer 20 sts from stitch holder to LH needle (the middle 12 sts remain on holder) and with RS facing rejoin yarn.

Row 18: Knit.

Row 19: P17, m1pl, P3. (21 sts)

Row 20: Knit.

Row 21: P18, K3.

Row 22 (buttonhole row): SSK, YO, knit to end.

Row 23: P16, SSP, K3. (20 sts)

Row 24: K3, SSK, knit to end. (19 sts)

Row 25: P14, SSP, K3. (18 sts)

Row 26 (buttonhole row): SSK, YO, K1, SSK, knit to end. (17 sts)

Row 27: K12, SSK, K3. (16 sts)

Row 28: K3, SSK, knit to end. (15 sts)

Row 29 (buttonhole row): K10, SSK, YO, K1, SSK. (14 sts)

Cast off.

CENTRE TONGUE

Transfer the remaining 12 sts from stitch holder to LH needle.

Row 18: With RS facing, pick up and knit the first 3 sts from the central edge behind the Left Side of sneaker (photo 1), K12, pick up and knit the first 3 sts from the central edge behind the Right Side of sneaker (photo 2). (18 sts)

Row 19: K2, P14, K2.

Row 20: K2, SSK, K10, K2tog, K2. (16 sts)

Row 21: K2, P12, K2.

Row 22: K2, SSK, K8, K2tog, K2. (14 sts)

Row 23: K2, P10, K2.

Row 24: Knit.

Rows 25–35: Rpt Rows 23-24 5 more times, then rpt Row 23 again.

Row 36: K1, SSK, K8, K2tog, K1. (12 sts)

Row 37: K1, K2tog, K6, SSK, K1. (10 sts)

Cast off.

LACES (MAKE 2)

Cast on 2 sts using 3mm dpns and the yarn specified for the outfit you are making.

Make an i-cord (see Techniques: Casting On and Stitches, Making i-cord), 105 rows long (31 cm/12⅜in).

MAKING UP

1. Sew the back edges of the sneaker together, working from the ankle down to the sole and to the toe.

2. Block the sneakers (the best way to do this is to shape the sneaker on the animal's foot, pull the sides in as if they were laced up and pin in place on the foot, then lightly steam).

3. Thread the laces through the buttonholes on each side of the sneaker (see photo).

MARY JANE SHOES

Knit the soles, as described in All Shoe Soles, then continue as follows:

LEFT SHOE

Change to the yarn specified in the outfit you are making.

Row 14: Purl.

Rows 15–22: Stocking stitch 8 rows.

Row 23: P16, P2tog 5 times, SSP 5 times, P16. (42 sts)

Row 24: K10, YO, K2, pass the YO st over the 2 knit sts (see photo 5 in T-Bar Shoes – this makes the beginning of the cast-off section much neater), cast off 19 sts starting with the second of the 'K2' sts (photo 6 in T-Bar Shoes), K12. This includes the st from the last cast off. (23 sts)

The top right and left sides of the shoe are now worked separately.

RIGHT SIDE

Work across the first 12 sts only.

Row 25: Knit.

Row 26: Cast on 9 sts using Purl cast-on method (see Techniques: Casting On and Stitches), K9, K2tog, knit to end. (20 sts)

Row 27 (buttonhole row): knit to last 3 sts, K2tog, YO, K1.

Cast off.

TIP

Don't forget to leave long tails when casting on and casting off. You can use these tails for sewing up the seams.

LEFT SIDE

With WS facing, rejoin yarn to remaining 11 sts.

Rows 25-27: Knit 3 rows.

Cast off.

RIGHT SHOE

Work as Rows 1–23 for Left Shoe.

Row 24: K11, YO, K2, pass the YO st over the 2 knit sts (see photo 5 in T-Bar Shoes – this makes the beginning of the cast-off section much neater), cast off 19 sts starting with the second of the 'K2' sts (photo 6 in T-Bar Shoes), K11. This includes the st from the last cast off. (23 sts)

The top right and left sides of the shoe are now worked separately.

RIGHT SIDE

Work across the first 11 sts only.

Rows 25-27: Knit 3 rows.

Cast off.

LEFT SIDE

Slip the remaining 12 sts onto opposite needle. With right sides facing, rejoin yarn to remaining 12 sts.

Row 25: Purl.

Row 26: Cast on 9 sts using Knit cast-on method (see Techniques: Casting On and Stitches), P9, SSP, purl to end. (20 sts)

Row 27 (buttonhole row): Purl to last 3 sts, P2tog, YO, P1.

Cast off purlwise.

MAKING UP

1. Sew the edges of the shoe together, working from the ankle down to the sole and then to the toe.

2. Sew button in place on opposite side of shoe to strap, lining it up with the buttonhole.

STARLET SHOES

Knit the soles, as described in All Shoe Soles, then continue as follows:

LEFT SHOE

Change to the yarn specified in the outfit you are making.

Rows 14–15: Purl 2 rows.

Row 16: K2, [YO, K3, pass 1st of the 3 knit sts over the 2nd and 3rd] to last 2 sts, K2.

Row 17: Purl.

Row 18: K1, [K3, pass 1st of the 3 knit sts over the 2nd and 3rd, YO] to last 3 sts, K3.

Rows 19-23: Rpt Rows 15-18 once more, then rpt Row 15 again.

Row 24: K10, YO, K2, pass the YO st over the 2 knit sts (photo 5 in T-Bar Shoes – this makes the beginning of the cast-off section much neater), K1, pass second of the 2 knit sts over st just worked (1st cast off), cast off last st worked and the following sts between * and * as you work them *K3, SSK 5 times, K2tog 5 times, K4*, K12. This includes the st from the last cast off. (23 sts)

The top right and left sides of the shoe are now worked separately.

RIGHT SIDE

Working across the first 12 sts only.

Row 25: Knit.

Row 26: Cast on 9 sts using Purl cast-on method (see Techniques: Casting On and Stitches), K9, K2tog, knit to end. (20 sts)

Row 27 (buttonhole row): Knit to last 3 sts, K2tog, YO, K1.

Cast off.

LEFT SIDE

With WS facing, rejoin yarn to remaining 11 sts.

Rows 25–27: Knit 3 rows.

Cast off.

RIGHT SHOE

Work Rows 1–23 as Left Shoe.

Row 24: K11, YO, K2, pass the YO st over the 2 knit sts (photo 5 in T-Bar Shoes – this makes the beginning of the cast-off section much neater), K1, pass second of the 2 knit sts over st just worked (1st cast off), cast off last st worked and the following sts between * and * as you work them *K2, SSK 5 times, K2tog 5 times, K5*, K11. This includes the st from the last cast off. (23 sts)

The top right and left sides of the shoe are now worked separately.

RIGHT SIDE

Working across the first 11 sts only.

Rows 25–27: Knit 3 rows.

Cast off.

LEFT SIDE

Slip the remaining 12 sts onto opposite needle. With RS facing, rejoin yarn to remaining 12 sts.

Row 25: Purl.

Row 26: Cast on 9 sts using Knit cast-on method (see Techniques: Casting On and Stitches), P9, SSP, purl to end. (20 sts)

Row 27 (buttonhole row): Purl to last 3 sts, P2tog, YO, P1.

Cast off purlwise.

MAKING UP

1. Sew the edges of the shoe together, working from the ankle down to the sole and to the toe.

2. Sew a button in place on opposite side of shoe to strap, lining it up with the buttonhole.

FRENCH KNICKERS

The knickers are worked top down with no seams. The top part is worked back and forth with a button band down the back and some short row shaping for the bottom; the lower half is worked in the round.

Using the yarn specified for the outfit you are making and 3mm straight needles, cast on 52 sts.

Row 1 (ws): Knit.

Row 2 (buttonhole row): K1, YO, K2tog, knit to end.

Row 3: Knit.

Change to 3.5mm straight needles.

Row 4: K1, [K2, K1fb] 4 times, [K1, K1fb] 13 times, [K2, K1fb] 3 times, K4. (72 sts)

Row 5: K2, P7, turn.

Row 6: YO, knit to end.

Row 7: K2, P7, SSP, P2, turn.

Row 8: YO, knit to end.

Row 9: K2, P10, SSP, P2, turn.

Row 10: YO, knit to end.

Row 11: K2, P13, SSP, P2, turn.

Row 12: YO, knit to end.

Row 13: K2, P16, SSP, purl to last 2 sts, K2.

Row 14: K9, turn.

Row 15: YO, purl to last 2 sts, K2.

Row 16: K9, K2tog, K2, turn.

Row 17: YO, purl to last 2 sts, K2.

Row 18: K12, K2tog, K2, turn.

Row 19 (buttonhole row): YO, purl to last 3 sts, P2tog, YO, K1.

Row 20: K15, K2tog, K2, turn.

Row 21: YO, purl to last 2 sts, K2.

Row 22: K18, K2tog, knit to end.

Row 23: K2, purl to last 2 sts, K2.

Row 24: Knit.

Row 25: K2, purl to last 2 sts, K2.

Row 26: K19, YO, SSK, K30, K2tog, YO, K19.

Row 27 (buttonhole row): K2, purl to last 3 sts, P2tog, YO, K1.

Row 28: K18, [YO, SSK] twice, K28, [K2tog, YO] twice, K18.

Row 29: K2, purl to last 2 sts, K2.

Row 30: K17, [YO, SSK] 3 times, K26, [K2tog, YO] 3 times, K17.

Row 31: K2, purl to last 2 sts, K2.

Row 32: Transfer sts to a 3.5mm circular needle, K16, [YO, SSK] 4 times, K24, [K2tog, YO] 4 times, knit to last 2 sts, slip the last 2 sts (without working them) onto a cable needle.

Join to work in the round:

Rnd 33: Position the cable needle behind the first 2 sts on the LH needle, knit first st on LH needle together with first st on cable needle, place marker for beginning of round, knit next st on LH needle together with remaining st on cable needle, knit to end. (70 sts)

Rnd 34: K14, [YO, SSK] 5 times, K22, [K2tog, YO] 5 times, K14.

Rnd 35: Knit.

Rnd 36: K1, m1l, K12, [YO, SSK] 6 times, K20, [K2tog, YO] 6 times, K12, m1r, K1. (72 sts)

Rnd 37: Knit

Rnd 38: K13, [YO, SSK] 7 times, K18, [K2tog, YO] 7 times, K13.

Rnd 39: K1, m1l, knit to last st, m1r, K1. (74 sts)

Rnd 40: K13, [YO, SSK] 8 times, K7, m1r, K2, m1l, K7, [K2tog, YO] 8 times, K13. (76 sts)

Rnd 41: K1, m1l, knit to last st, m1r, K1. (78 sts)

Rnd 42: K13, [YO, SSK] 9 times, K16, [K2tog, YO] 9 times, K13.

Rnd 43: K1, m1l, K37, m1r, K2, m1l, K37, m1r, K1. (82 sts)

Rnd 44: K13, [YO, SSK] 10 times, K16, [K2tog, YO] 10 times, K13.

Rnd 45: K1, m1l, K39, m1r, K2, m1l, K39, m1r, K1. (86 sts)

Rnd 46: K13, [YO, SSK] 11 times, K16, [K2tog, YO] 11 times, K13.

Divide for legs:

Rnd 47: K43 (right leg), without working them place next 43 sts onto waste yarn (left leg).

RIGHT LEG

Change to 3mm circular needle.

Rnd 48: K12, [YO, SSK] 12 times, K7.

Rnd 49: Purl.

Rnd 50: Knit.

Rnd 51: Purl.

Cast off.

LEFT LEG

Rnd 47: Transfer sts from waste yarn to 3.5mm circular needle, rejoin yarn and knit 1 rnd placing marker for beginning of rnd.

Change to 3mm circular needle.

Rnd 48: K7, [K2tog, YO] 12 times, K12.

Rnd 49: Purl.

Rnd 50: Knit.

Rnd 51: Purl.

Cast off.

MAKING UP

1. If necessary, close hole with a couple of stitches where the 2 legs join.

2. Block knickers.

3. Sew buttons in place on left-hand button band down back of knickers, matching them up with the buttonholes.

TECHNIQUES

MAKING UP YOUR ANIMAL

The animals all share common features and techniques in their assembly. In this section you'll find everything you need to know about completing your animal's head, body, arms and legs.

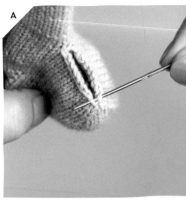

For all the animals please bear the following in mind when assembling their parts:

Where possible use the cast-on/cast-off tails for sewing up. Tie off or weave in any other loose ends as you go.

Use a tapestry needle and mattress stitch (unless otherwise indicated) for sewing up seams.

After sewing parts together bury loose ends inside the body.

BODY

1. Starting at the bottom, thread yarn tail through the cast-on stitches and gather up, then sew edges together stopping about 6cm (2⅜in) up from the centre bottom, but do not fasten off just yet.

2. Now working down from the neck, sew the top half of the back seam together leaving a gap (about 5cm/2in) to push stuffing through.

3. Stuff body (you are aiming for the body to measure about 25cm (10in) around its widest point) and, still working from the top down, close the gap. When you reach the bottom half of the seam, knot both yarn ends securely and bury them inside the body, pulling tightly so the knot goes through to the wrong side of the fabric.

LEGS

TOP OF FOOT

Start by sewing the cast-off edges along the top of the foot together:

1. Using the same yarn as the foot and working from right to left, insert a threaded tapestry needle through the

outer loops of the cast-off stitches either side of the centre stitch at the front of the foot, pull yarn through leaving a short tail to weave in (A).

2. Insert needle through outer loop of stitch just worked on right-hand edge and next stitch up on opposite edge, pull yarn through (B).

3. Insert needle through outer loop of next stitch on each edge and pull yarn through (C).

4. Repeat step 3 for each remaining cast-off stitch (D).

5. To finish, working in an anti-clockwise direction insert needle under the 'V' of the next stitch on the right-hand side, centre and left side, then down through the centre seam to wrong side of work (E).

FOOT PAD AND LEGS

1. Sew the bottom edges of the foot together, starting at the front of the foot pad working through to the ankle.

2. Stuff the foot firmly.

3. Sew the leg edges together, stuffing as you go. Only lightly stuff the top part of the legs to enable them to move and dangle nicely.

SEWING THE LEGS TO THE BODY

Matching the top of the legs with the leg position marks on the body and with the leg seam central to the back of the leg, sew the legs to the body using mattress stitch (see Casting On and Stitches). Sew the front half of the legs to the first row of stitches above the position marks and the back half of the legs to the first row immediately below the position marks.

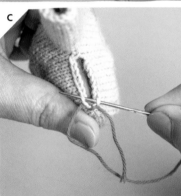

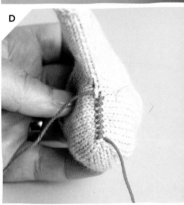

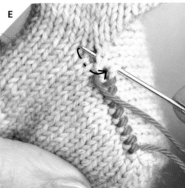

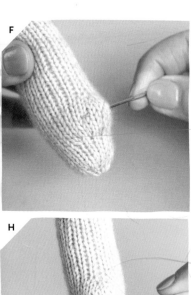

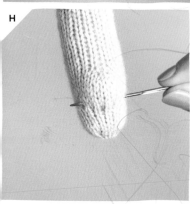

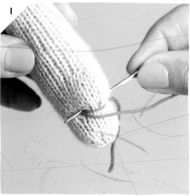

TIP

When stuffing your animal, use small pieces of toy stuffing. Roll and manipulate the body parts in your hands to spread the stuffing evenly and ensure a smooth shape. Tease out lumps using a blunt tapestry needle carefully inserted through the knitting between the stitches.

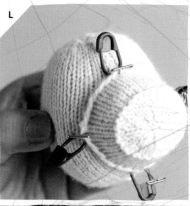

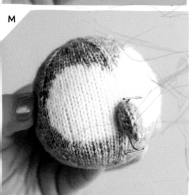

ARMS

1. Starting at the gathered end of the hand, sew the side edges together, stuffing as you go. Stuff the hand and first ⅓ of the arm quite firmly, shaping the thumb by teasing out the stuffing with a tapestry needle (F). Then gradually decrease the amount of stuffing as you work up the arm, with no stuffing at the very top (G).

2. To define the thumb, sew through the hand and over the top of the thumb a couple of times with a long stitch (H and I).

3. Sew arms in position on each side of body, roughly 3cm (1¼in) down from centre of neck and with thumbs facing forward.

HEAD

1. Starting at the top, sew the edges together, leaving a big enough gap at the bottom to push the stuffing through.

2. Stuff head firmly and close the gap, finish by threading the yarn through the cast-on stitches and draw up.

3. Using scraps of cotton 4-ply yarn, embroider the nose details onto your animal's face (for the animals with a beak or a snout please see Beaks and Snout section). To secure, knot both yarn ends securely and bury them inside the head, pulling tightly so the knot goes through to the wrong side of the fabric.

For the Ram - *Using a few loose stitches, embroider two mini bobbles on top of the ram's head along the seam line to fill the gap (J).*

BEAKS AND SNOUT

1. Sew edges of beak/snout together, starting at the drawn up stitches working towards the cast-on edge and making sure any colour changes match up.

2. Stuff beak/snout.

3. Position on face and pin in place.

For the Duck - *Match up the top point, side slip stitch detail and bottom seam with the four markers on head (K).*

For the Pig - *Centralise the snout within the four markers on head, making sure the seam is at the bottom (L).*

For the Owl - *With seam at the bottom, centralise the beak at the start of the contrast colour of face (M).*

4. Sew the beak/snout to face using the Half mattress stitch method (see Techniques: Casting On and Stitches).

EYES

1. Using a long sewing needle and a double sewing thread, sew eye buttons in position on either side of head; sew both buttons on at the same time, sewing through the head and pulling them in slightly to indent the face (see main photo of animal in each project for eye position).

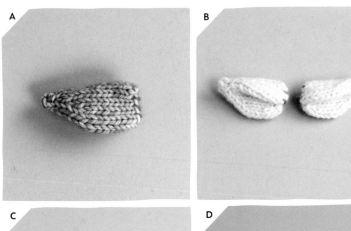

EARS

1. Fold the ears along both lines of decrease stitches so the edges are at the centre back.

2. Sew the edges together, starting at the gathered stitches working down towards the cast-on end.

3. Now follow the instructions below for Hare, Horse, Squirrel, Ram and Pig. For the other animals go straight to step 4.

For the Hare, Horse and Squirrel - Fold ears in half with the back on the outside and the front halves touching and over sew the bottom edges together to keep in place (A).

For the Ram - Lay the ears flat with fronts facing you and the cast-on ends facing each other, and then fold the top half of each ear over so it doesn't quite meet the edge of the bottom half. Over sew the cast-on edges together to keep in place (B).

For the Pig - Lay the ears flat with fronts facing you and the cast-on ends facing each other, fold the top 2cm (¾in) of each ear down and the bottom 1cm (½in) of each ear up. Secure with a couple of small stitches (C).

4. Pin ears in place on animal's head (see main photo of animal in project for positions) and sew in place.

For the Hare, Horse, Squirrel and Ram's ears, take your tapestry needle under the stitches on the head (D) and then right through the bottom of each ear (E).

For the other animals, attach the ears to the head by sewing around the bottom of the ear using the Half mattress stitch method (see Techniques: Casting On and Stitches).

For the Dog - As a final step, fold the ears over and secure the inner front edge of the ear to the face with a stitch about 15mm (⅝in) up from the tip of the ear (F).

HORSE'S MANE

1. Sew the cast-off end of each i-cord into position, along the top and down the seam at the back of the horse's head (G).

2. Thread the loose cast-on tail through the middle of the i-cord and bury inside the head.

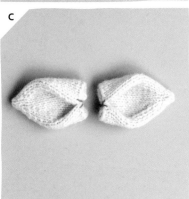

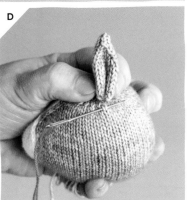

RAM'S HORNS

1. Sew the edges of the horn together, starting at the drawn up stitches and working towards the cast-on edge, stuffing as you go.

2. Position horns on each side of the head, pin in place (H and I).

3. Sew onto the head using Half mattress stitch (see Techniques: Casting On and Stitches).

4. Gently manipulate the horn so it curls around the ear and secure it to the head with a small stitch (J).

TAILS

CAT, DOG, DUCK, FOX, MOUSE, PIG, RACCOON AND SQUIRREL

1. Sew the edges of the tail together, starting at the drawn up stitches, working towards the cast-on edge and making sure any colour changes match up, stuffing as you go (see instructions below for Cat's tail).

For Cat's tail only - In order to curl the cat's tail slightly, before sewing the edges together secure a long length of matching yarn just above the cream tip. Run this up the centre of the WS, threading it through the back loop of the centre stitch on every 4th row (K) (you don't need to be exact). Poke through to the right side of the tail when you reach the top. Once you have seamed and stuffed the tail, use this thread to draw up and shape the tail, then fasten off securely and bury inside the body.

2. Position the tail on the back of the body, centring it on the back seam and with the centre of the tail 6cm (2⅜in) up from the centre of the gathered cast-on stitches on the underneath of the body; pin in place.

3. Sew the tail onto the body using Half mattress stitch (see Techniques: Casting On and Stitches).

HARE

1. Sew the pompom onto the back of the hare's body, centring it on the back seam and with the centre of the pompom 6cm (2⅜in) up from the middle of the gathered cast-on stitches on the underneath of the body (L).

HORSE

1. Starting with the shortest at the top, position the i-cords in size order (M) and sew them together at one end.

2. Stitch the tail to the horse's body, centring it on the back seam and with the centre of the tail 6cm (2⅜in) up from the middle of the gathered cast-on stitches on the underneath of the body.

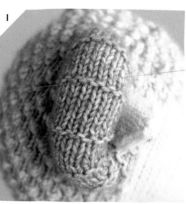

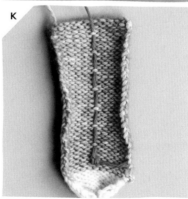

TIP

To make sure all the items of clothing fit neatly round the tails, it is important to make sure the tails are centred 6cm (2⅜in) up from the gathered stitches on the underneath of the body.

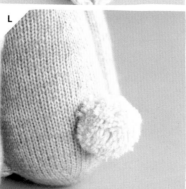

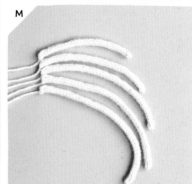

CASTING ON AND STITCHES

In the following pages I've gathered all the cast-on methods that I use, as well as step-by-step guides to the stitches you'll need to complete your animal friends.

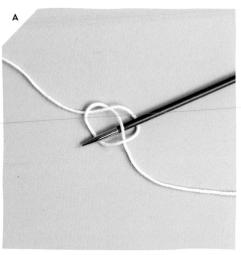

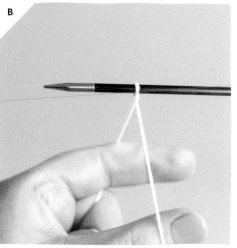

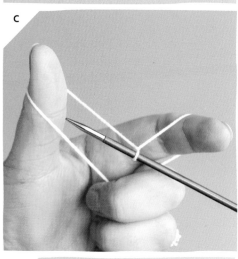

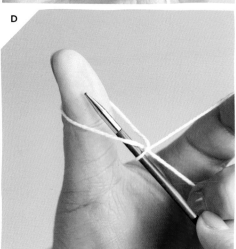

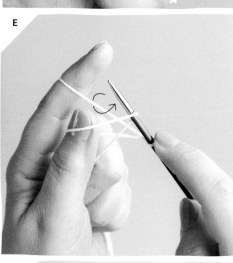

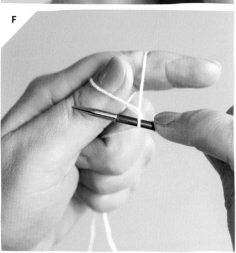

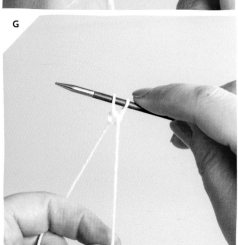

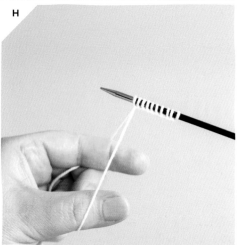

LONG TAIL CAST-ON

(Also known as double cast-on.)

To make sure you have a long enough tail to cast on your stitches, wrap the yarn around the needle the same amount of times as the amount of stitches you need plus about 25cm (10in) extra to use for sewing up later if needed.

1. Make a slip knot (A).

2. With the needle in your right hand, keeping the ball end closest to you, place your left thumb and forefinger between the two strands of yarn. Grasp the loose ends with your other fingers and hold them in your palm (B).

3. Spread your thumb and forefinger apart to make the yarn taut, then move your thumb up towards the tip of the needle, keeping your palm facing forwards (C).

4. Bring the tip of the needle up through the loop on your thumb (D).

5. Then over the top and around the yarn on your forefinger (E).

6. Take the needle back through the thumb loop (insert from top) (F).

7. Gently pull your thumb out and pull on tail ends to tighten the stitch (G).

8. Repeat steps 3–7 (H).

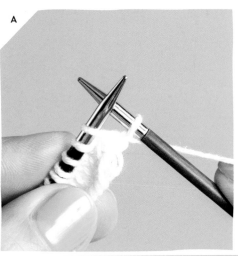

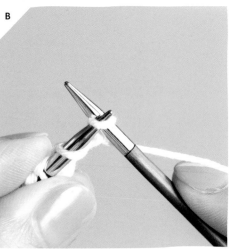

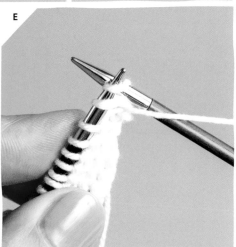

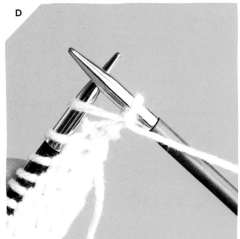

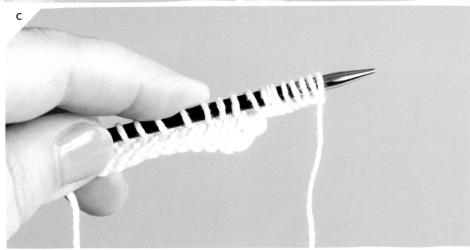

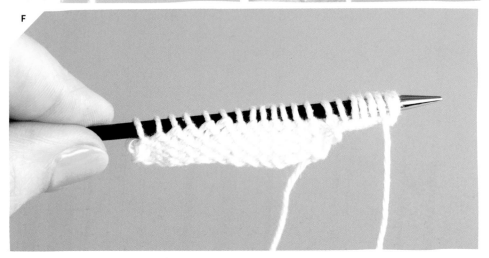

KNIT CAST-ON

1. Insert the right needle into the first stitch on the left needle and knit, but do not take the left-hand stitch off the needle (A).

2. Transfer the loop from the right needle to the left by inserting the left needle up through the bottom of the loop (B).

3. Repeat steps 1 and 2 (C).

PURL CAST-ON

1. Insert the right needle into the first stitch on left needle and purl, but do not take the left-hand stitch off the needle (D).

2. Transfer the loop from the right needle to the left by inserting the left needle up through the bottom of the loop (E).

3. Repeat steps 1 and 2 (F).

PICKING UP STITCHES

BEHIND BUTTON BAND OR VENT

You need to be picking up the stitches on the same row as the live stitches on the left-hand needle; the easiest way to find the correct row on the right-hand piece of fabric is to follow across the row below the one you need:

1. With right side facing, fold the right-hand side of the work over slightly so you can see the wrong side of the fabric (G), follow the first row of purl bumps directly under the live stitches on the LH needle across to the RH piece of work (H). Working from left to right and starting with the purl bump after the first stitch on LH needle count one purl bump for each picked up stitch required (I). The first stitch you need to pick up is the purl bump directly under this.

2. Insert the right-hand needle up through the purl bump directly below the one you counted to (J), wrap yarn around needle and pull through as if to knit.

3. Insert right needle up through the purl bump of the next stitch, wrap yarn around needle and pull through as if to knit. Repeat this step until the required number of stitches have been picked up and knitted (K).

AROUND NECK

1. With the stated side facing (see pattern) and working from right to left, insert the right-hand needle up through the horizontal loop of the first required cast-on stitch (L).

2. Wrap the yarn around the needle and pull through as if to knit (M).

3. Insert the right-hand needle up through the horizontal loop of the next cast-on stitch (N).

4. Repeat steps 2 and 3 until the required number of stitches have been worked.

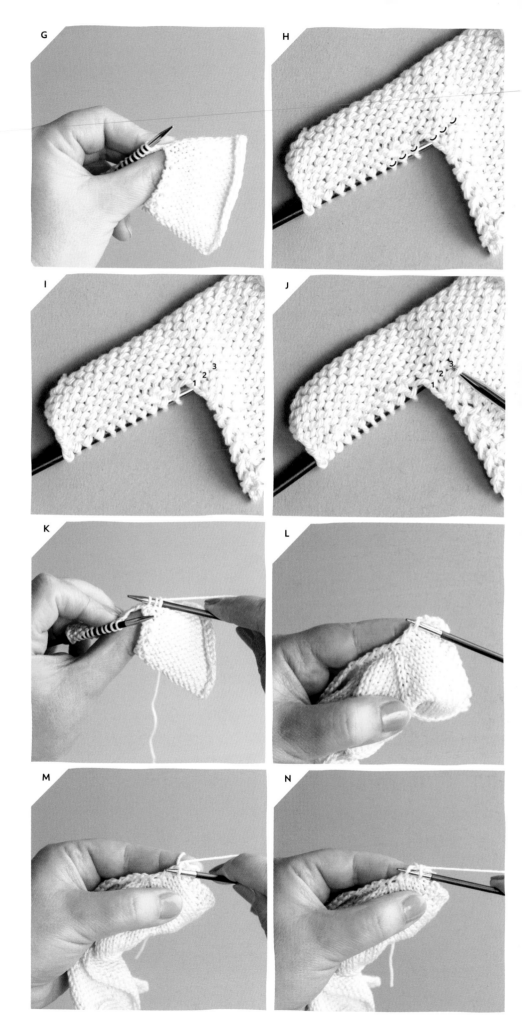

A

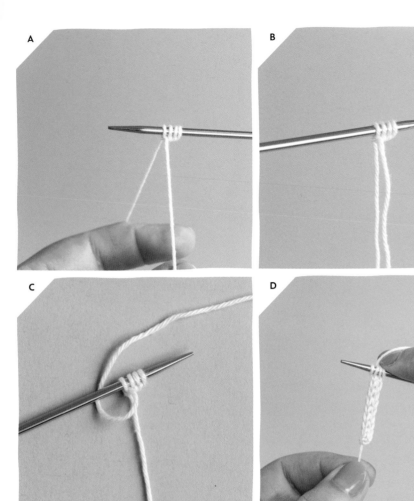

B

C

D

E

F

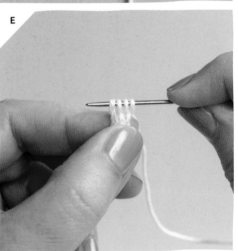
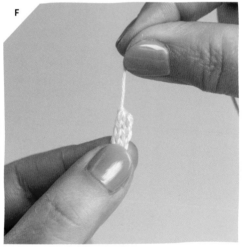

MAKING I-CORD

Worked on two double-pointed needles.

1. Cast on the number of stitches needed using Long Tail Cast-On (A).

2. Without turning your work, slide the stitches to the right-hand end of the needle (B).

3. Bringing the working yarn around the back (C), knit the first stitch, pulling the yarn tight and knit to the end of the row.

4. Repeat steps 2 and 3 until the required length is reached, tugging on the cast-on tail after every row to form into a tube (D).

5. To cast off, cut the yarn and thread the tail end onto a tapestry needle; carefully slide stitches off the knitting needle and working from right to left push tapestry needle with yarn tail through the stitches and draw up (E and F).

MATTRESS STITCH

Thread the tail (or a length of yarn) onto a tapestry needle. Start with the right sides up and edges side by side.

VERTICAL MATTRESS STITCH

This stitch is used for seaming two selvedge edges together.

1. Insert the needle up through the first cast-on or cast-off loop on the opposite piece, then do the same on the first piece and pull the yarn through (G and H).

2. Take the needle across to the opposite edge again and insert from the front under two horizontal bars in the middle of the outermost stitches (I).

3. Repeat step 2, working back and forth across each side, gently pulling the yarn through to close the seam (J).

HORIZONTAL MATTRESS STITCH

This stitch is used for seaming the cast-on or cast-off edges together.

1. Insert the needle under the 'V' of the first stitch and pull the yarn through (K).

2. Take the needle across to the other edge and do the same with the stitch on that side (L).

3. Repeat steps 1 and 2, working back and forth across each side, gently pulling the yarn through to close the seam (M).

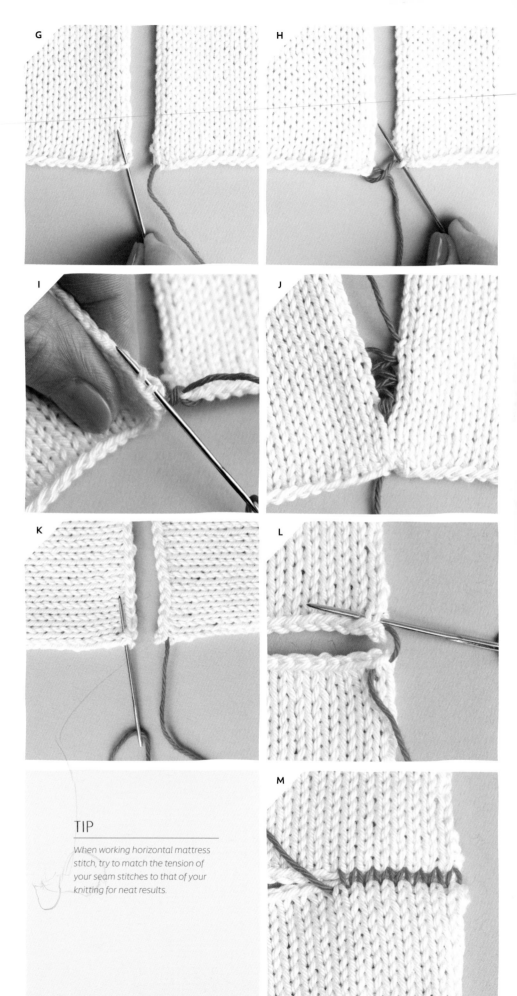

TIP

When working horizontal mattress stitch, try to match the tension of your seam stitches to that of your knitting for neat results.

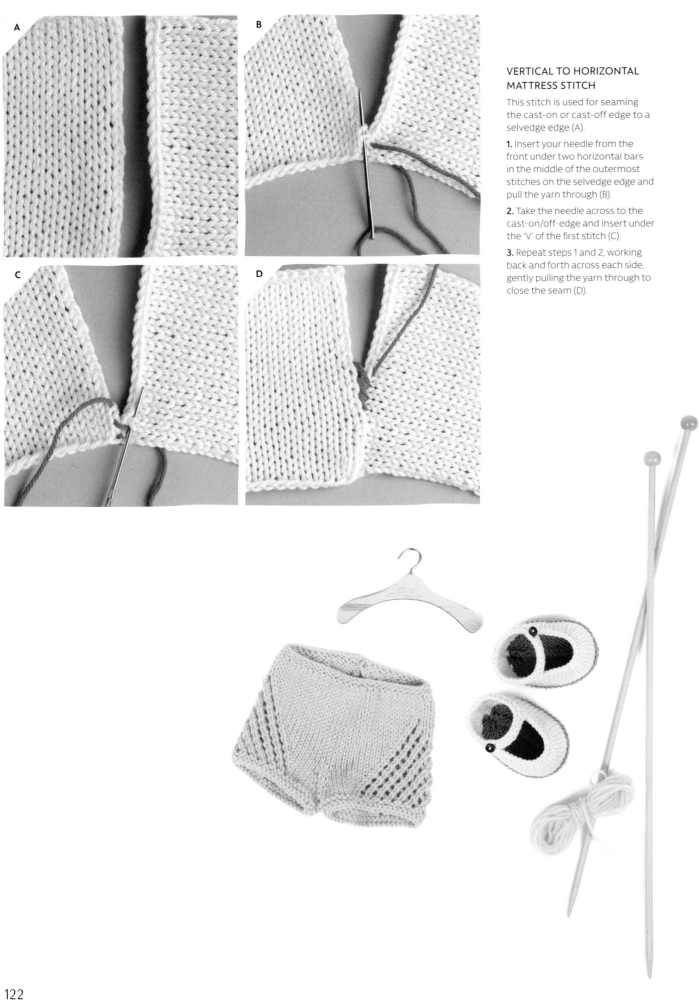

A

B

C

D

VERTICAL TO HORIZONTAL MATTRESS STITCH

This stitch is used for seaming the cast-on or cast-off edge to a selvedge edge (A).

1. Insert your needle from the front under two horizontal bars in the middle of the outermost stitches on the selvedge edge and pull the yarn through (B).

2. Take the needle across to the cast-on/off-edge and insert under the 'V' of the first stitch (C).

3. Repeat steps 1 and 2, working back and forth across each side, gently pulling the yarn through to close the seam (D).

HALF MATTRESS STITCH

This stitch is used for attaching some of the animals' ears, beaks, snout and tails onto the head and body.

1. Thread the tail end (or length of matching yarn) onto a tapestry needle.

2. Insert your needle up through the first cast-on loop of piece you are attaching and pull the yarn through (E).

3. Insert the needle down through the next cast-on loop of the piece and pull the yarn through (F).

4. Insert the needle under the 'V' of the stitch or under two horizontal bars (depending on the direction you are sewing) on the head/body and pull yarn through (G and H).

5. Insert the needle back up the last cast-on loop you worked and pull the yarn through (I).

6. Repeat steps 3-5 (J).

BLOCKING

Blocking your work will help to create a flat, neat finish and help stop edges from curling. Use rust-proof pins and leave to dry completely before removing pins. You can use spray blocking or steam blocking with cotton yarn.

SPRAY BLOCKING

Spray the knitted piece with cold water until it is damp but not saturated. Pin flat, and leave to dry completely.

STEAM BLOCKING

Pin the knitted piece flat and hold a steam iron close to the fabric and steam until it is damp (do not touch the fabric with the iron). Leave to dry.

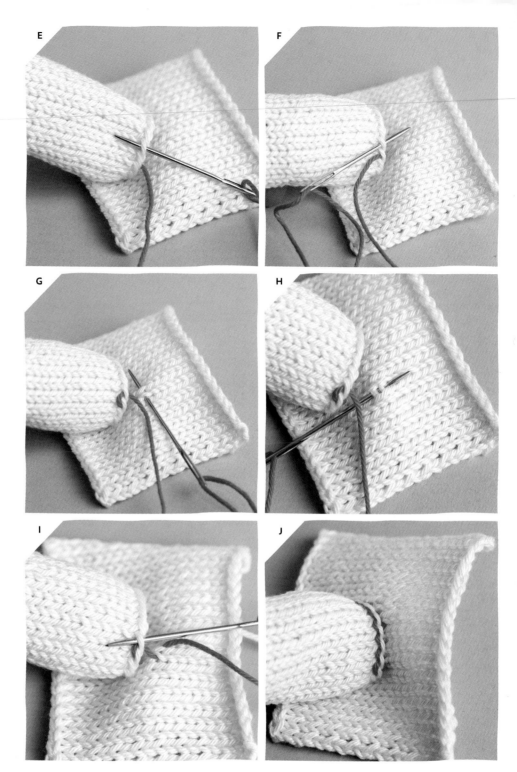

COLOURWORK

Most of the animals and their outfits use some sort of colour changing techniques, so I've collected my advice here. You'll find instructions on working stripes, Fair Isle and Intarsia, which you will need in order to create some of the animals and the decorated sweaters in this book. But don't worry, colourwork is easier than it looks!

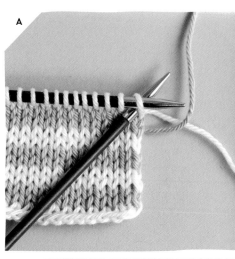

STRIPES

When working stripes, carry the yarn up the side of the work. Simply drop the old colour at the back of the work and pick up the new colour to work the first stitch (A). For thicker stripes (more than four rows) catch the old yarn every couple of rows by twisting it with the working yarn (B).

FAIR ISLE (STRANDED)

Fair Isle is a technique for working two (or more) colours of yarn in the same row, carrying the yarn at the back of the work. As you change colours simply let the old yarn hang down at the back of the work until needed again and pick up the new yarn to work the next stitch. If the strand of yarn being carried at the back of the yarn (the 'float') is longer than four stitches, twist the floating yarn around the working yarn by bringing it up over the top of the working yarn and down the back again. Try not to pull too tightly when changing colours (C and D).

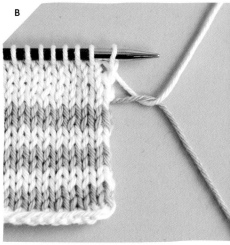

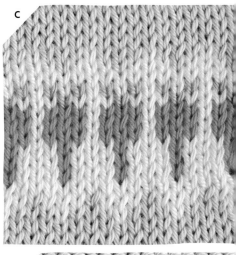

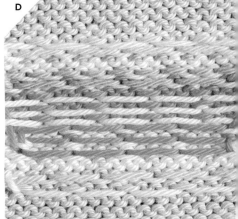

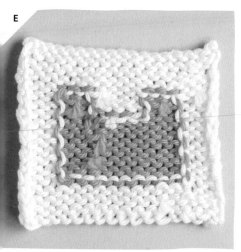

E

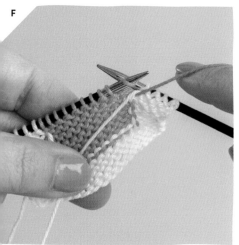

F

INTARSIA

Intarsia uses separate lengths or balls of yarn for each area of colour (as opposed to yarns being carried at the back of the work) (E). Although, if there is only one stitch between two areas of the same colour, the same length of yarn can be used for both and carried across the back of the single stitch.

It is best to work out how many changes of colour there are before starting and wind the longer lengths of yarn onto separate bobbins or clothes pegs.

For example, to work this sample chart you would need three lengths of cream yarn and two lengths of orange yarn. When following a chart, work from the bottom to the top and read knit rows (RS) from right to left and purl rows (WS) from left to right. This sample chart is worked in stocking stitch and the first row is a knit row, therefore you would begin reading it from the bottom right-hand corner.

An easy way to estimate how much yarn is needed is to count the number of stitches on the chart for each additional yarn length required. Loosely wrap the yarn around your needle once for each stitch then add a further 15cm (6in) for each tail.

To avoid holes between two blocks of colour, work until you need to change colour. Put the needle in the next stitch ready to work it, but pull the old yarn to the left before bringing the new colour yarn up and over it to work the stitch (F).

TIP

To tighten up any loose stitches once finished, working on the right side of the fabric, insert a tapestry needle into one leg of the loose stitch and pull towards you gently. Repeat on the next few stitches to even out the tension (G).

G

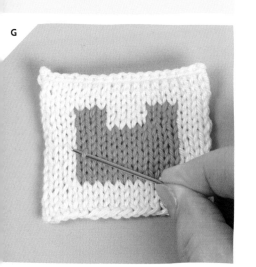

INTARSIA CHART

1	Cream yarn, length 1.
2	Cream yarn, length 2.
3	Cream yarn, length 3.
1	Orange yarn, length 1.
2	Orange yarn, length 2.

2	2	2	1	1	1	3	3	3	3	2	2	2	1	1	1
2	2	2	1	1	1	3	3	3	3	2	2	2	1	1	1
2	2	2	1	1	1	3	3	3	3	2	2	2	1	1	1
2	2	2	1	1	1	1	1	1	1	1	1	1	1	1	1
2	2	2	1	1	1	1	1	1	1	1	1	1	1	1	1
2	2	2	1	1	1	1	1	1	1	1	1	1	1	1	1
2	2	2	1	1	1	1	1	1	1	1	1	1	1	1	1
2	2	2	1	1	1	1	1	1	1	1	1	1	1	1	1
2	2	2	1	1	1	1	1	1	1	1	1	1	1	1	1
2	2	2	1	1	1	1	1	1	1	1	1	1	1	1	1

SUPPLIERS

BOO-BILOO
www.boobiloo.co.uk

SEWANDSO
www.sewandso.co.uk

SCHEEPJES
www.scheepjes.com

LOVEKNITTING
www.loveknitting.com

WOOL WAREHOUSE
www.woolwarehouse.co.uk

DERAMORES
www.deramores.com

THANKS

A big thank you to the team at F&W Media for making this book possible, and to Jane and Lynne for all your hard work.

Thanks also to my family and friends for all your enthusiasm and encouragement, your constant support has been invaluable.

Finally, the biggest thank you has to go to my husband Kevin, who, as always, has been my tower of strength.

ABOUT THE AUTHOR

Louise's love of knitting started when her eldest son came home from school one day saying he wanted to learn how to knit... his interest in knitting lasted about a week, but she has been hooked ever since!

Louise, who has a background in textile design, has developed her own successful brand, Boo-Biloo, selling knitting patterns for toys and dolls. Her work has been featured in various craft and knitting magazines, and in her previous book, *My Knitted Doll*.

To find out more about Louise's work visit her at:

www.boobiloo.co.uk

www.facebook.com/boobiloo

www.instagram.com/boo_biloo

INDEX

A SEWANDSO BOOK
© F&W Media International, Ltd 2019

SewandSo is an imprint of F&W Media International, Ltd
Pynes Hill Court, Pynes Hill, Exeter, EX2 5AZ, UK

F&W Media International, Ltd is a subsidiary of F+W Media, Inc
10151 Carver Road, Suite #200, Blue Ash, OH 45242, USA

Text and Designs © Louise Crowther 2019
Layout and Photography © F&W Media International, Ltd 2019

First published in the UK and USA in 2019

Louise Crowther has asserted her right to be identified as author of this
work in accordance with the Copyright, Designs and Patents Act, 1988.

A catalogue record for this book is available from the British Library.

ISBN-13: 978-1-4463-0731-1 paperback
SRN: R9320 paperback

ISBN-13: 978-1-4463-7756-7 PDF
SRN: R9949 PDF

ISBN-13: 978-1-4463-7755-0 EPUB
SRN: R9948 EPUB

Printed in Slovenia for:
F&W Media International, Ltd
Pynes Hill Court, Pynes Hill, Exeter, EX2 5AZ, UK

10 9 8 7 6 5 4 3 2 1

Content Director: Ame Verso
Acquisitions Editor: Sarah Callard
Managing Editor: Jeni Hennah
Project Editor: Jane Trollope
Pattern Checker: Lynne Rowe
Design Manager: Anna Wade
Designers: Anna Wade, Sam Staddon, Lorraine Inglis and Ali Stark
Art Direction: Prudence Rogers
Photographer: Jason Jenkins
Production Manager: Beverley Richardson

F&W Media publishes high quality books on a wide range of subjects.
For more great book ideas visit: www.sewandso.co.uk

Layout of the digital edition of this book may vary depending on reader
hardware and display settings.